INSTITUTE OF LEADERSHIP & MANAGEMENT (ILM)
THE PROFESSIONAL INSTITUTE OF CHOICE FOR TODAY'S MANAGER

Founded over 50 years ago and now part of the City & Guilds Group, the Institute of Leadership & Management (ILM) is unique among professional bodies. As the largest awarding body for management – related qualifications with over 75,000 candidates each year, the ILM recognises and fosters good management practice. As a professional body, ILM also offers informal personal and professional support to practising leaders and managers across all disciplines and at every career stage.

20,000 members have already found that ILM membership gives them the strategic, ongoing support they need to fulfil their aims, enabling them to enhance their skills, add to their professional expertise and to develop a wider network of valuable business contacts.

For further information on becoming a member of ILM please contact the Membership Department on telephone + 44 (0) 1543 251 346. www.i-l-m.com

Practical Leadership

GORDON MACKAY

Chandos Publishing
Oxford · England

Published in association with

Institute of Leadership
& Management

Chandos Publishing (Oxford) Limited
Chandos House
5 & 6 Steadys Lane
Stanton Harcourt
Oxford OX29 5RL
UK
Tel: +44 (0) 1865 884447 Fax: +44 (0) 1865 884448
Email: info@chandospublishing.com
www.chandospublishing.com

First published in Great Britain in 2006

ISBN:
1 84334 209 X (paperback)
1 84334 210 3 (hardback)
978 1 84334 209 0 (paperback)
978 1 84334 210 6 (hardback)

© G. MacKay, 2006

British Library Cataloguing-in-Publication Data.
A catalogue record for this book is available from the British Library.

Typeset by Domex e-Data Pvt. Ltd.
Printed in the UK and USA.

Contents

Preface

This book constitutes a distillation of insights born of successful leadership practice over many years. Personal, historical and contemporary examples richly illustrate and reinforce the hard-won, practical guidance it offers to all who study, or follow, the leadership path.

Based primarily on the 'lived experience' of leadership, it may be seen as a bridge between academic models, theories, 'multi-national case-studies', etc., and the 'real world' of leadership-in-practice. The book's primary target though is those considering, or taking on, for the very first time, the many challenges of practical leadership.

In retrospect, I came to realise that my own path to leadership took place over many years during which I observed, was subject to and in some cases was 'subjected' to the 'leadership' of others: first by Royal Naval officers during my engineering apprenticeship, and subsequently in civilian industry and commerce.

During my youth, along with countless others, I thrilled to tales of outstanding leadership: of figures like Sir Ernest Shackleton in the Antarctic, Field Marshall Sir William Slim in Burma (Myanmar) and, more recently, who can fail to be impressed and stirred by the qualities of self-leadership demonstrated so ably and courageously by Dame Ellen Macarthur as she sailed round the world, faster than any man, or woman – ever?

I was and often still am stirred and inspired by these romantic images of leadership found in movies, books and even in 'real life'. Such portrayals of leadership attracted me to the role of leadership by firing my imagination to believe that perhaps I too could 'make a difference'.

The absence of opportunities actually to experience leadership for myself though made any possibility of it ever occurring seem sometimes unimaginably remote. Yet as I grew and reflected upon others' leadership in real life, I was quietly reassured by my discovery that in the real world, leaders were often actually no more 'clever' or knowledgeable than I. This deepening awareness quietly and gradually fuelled a growing conviction that I too could lead, given the opportunity. It also fed my desire to learn from my own experiences of being led, both good and bad, such that if and when I was ever called upon to lead, I would have a valuable store of knowledge gained by steady observation and reflection to draw upon.

With time, I also learned that leadership requires far more than technical or 'expert' knowledge, whatever the field of endeavour. A fundamental source of any leader's ability to lead, I realised, depends upon their knowledge and understanding of themselves, their team as a whole and each individual in it.

Technical knowledge of a project is vital for management, but leadership is dynamic; it emerges in action as a 'competence', as something 'lived and breathed'. Leadership success often seemed to turn on how one is perceived. Leadership credibility, like an actor's, shines *through* the 'outward' roles they fulfil.

In time, I came to understand that such dynamic leadership competence is invariably built upon the unremitting exercise of self-leadership and self-assurance. It is not purely genetic, though some are undoubtedly 'gifted' to some degree. But that one can *develop* competent leadership skills, and achieve great success as a leader whether 'gifted' or not, is a fact proven time and again by history. Such leadership qualities are nurtured through the rigorous exercise of reflexivity, self-discipline and self-motivation.

As graduate and MBA student, I often wondered why the books on leadership I was given to study focused on the work of a corporate chief, or senior executives, despite the fact that the majority studying practical leadership, and needing its basic skills, may not even aspire to, never mind reach, such exalted positions for many years. This book seeks consciously to address this gap by focusing upon *practical* issues of leadership: how one prepares for and exercises day-to-day leadership effectively.

Being unexpectedly catapulted into the leadership experience I went from having practically no experience in leadership at all, to being responsible for leading more than 320 staff, across multiple disciplines and functions. I then 'turned-round' a call centre, employing over a thousand employees, from being rated worst of 13 centres, to being Best of Breed: Number One. This I saw achieved in just 4 months.

With such experience to draw upon, I believe I have something of value to offer aspiring leaders, those facing its challenges, opportunities, responsibilities and, as shall be seen, its 'loneliness' for the first time.

I acknowledge gratefully and without reserve that my successes would and could not have happened without the active engagement of many individuals from around the world who worked with and around me. All I did, in the end, was help them realise something of their *own* potential, for it was they, after all, who did the work successfully! Yet here stands one of the 'mysteries' of leadership to be explored in what follows; how does one become and remain a leader capable of releasing the potential of so many?

The path of leadership is a journey almost anyone can make.

It is an adventure almost anyone can embark upon.

But it is not 'a job'.

What 'makes the difference', defines and forges the leader, is their willingness to take the first 'steps to leadership'; these occur not in any public arena but silently, and unobserved, within. These first steps are nowhere documented more vividly or perhaps more surprisingly than the earliest stories we ever heard. One such example providing insight on the path to leadership is to be found in the Russian fairy tale known as *The Firebird*.

The Firebird

It begins, as do many classical myths, with a metaphorical door to adventure and personal growth being presented, offered, even, depending on your point of view, 'thrust-upon' the unwitting adventurer. This is the *'hero's'* first challenge: a decision whether to embrace the adventure or turn aside ...

A young warrior travels through the forest on horseback. Suddenly he becomes aware; the birds and creatures of the forest have all fallen eerily silent.

Nature itself seems to hold its breath.

Rounding a bend they see, lying before them upon the path, a single brilliant fiery feather.

From this crimson gold and fluttering flame they cannot move their eyes, as deep within them, another leaps to life ...

The horse now speaks, as of course they may in such stories: 'Behold, lying on the path before us, is a feather from the fabulous Firebird!'

The adventurer smiles; bringing such a gift to the King will surely afford great honour, riches and maybe more ... But then, breaking into the adventurer's happy reverie, as if reading his mind, the horse speaks once more: 'Go ahead, pick up the feather if you desire favour from your King. Be warned though, to pick up *this* feather will lead you to learn the meaning of "Fear", "Danger" and "Trouble such as you never guessed could be ..."'

'On the other hand', says the horse, turning to look the adventurer in the eye, 'this one small action would carry you to many unimaginable adventures, not least to meeting the King' ...

Would *you* pick up the Firebird's feather?

This is where leadership starts: with solitary decisions; with no certain outcome, no guarantees of 'happy ever after'; a willingness and genuine lasting commitment to accept the threats and challenges, as well as the opportunities the path presents.

The myth of the Firebird is ancient, yet even today, if we are prepared to listen, we may still sense those moments when the 'the creatures of the forest fall silent'. We may recognise, too, within those silent moments the drift and fall of a fiery feather upon the path before us; our own 'Summons to Adventure'.

We may recognise it and may choose to lift that almost weightless feather that yet changes our life irrevocably. Such moments define us as they reveal our ability and willingness to recognise and act upon them.

Leadership begins then with self-leadership. Uniquely in such moments of decision we forge the very characteristics that set the leader apart from those who follow.

The greatest heights both reached and kept,
Were not by sudden flight achieved
For they while their companions slept
Were toiling upwards through the night! (Henry
Wadsworth Longfellow)

About the author

Gordon MacKay is an experienced management consultant and project manager and has successfully led an organisation of over a thousand employees to being externally assessed as the best in its field.

From his initial professional training as a Royal Naval engineer he has been fascinated by the experience and exercise of leadership. A desire to inform his own lack of direct leadership experience prompted him, as outlined in this book, to achieve a Degree in Organisation Studies and then an MBA with the Open University. These academic qualifications were then informed through experience as a Senior Consultant and Project Manager with a major international IT management consultancy. His desire to seek out an opportunity to experience practical man management and leadership first hand led to the experiences outlined here.

Gordon has also practised throughout the Highlands as a professionally qualified senior management Assessor and Mentor on the National Vocational Qualification (NVQ) programme.

Believing that guidance for first-time leaders is often obscured behind theories far removed from the day-to-day practice of leadership, his approach is based on the conviction that leadership is open to all willing to embrace its challenges and accompanying responsibilities.

The author may be contacted by telephone or e-mail:

Tel.: +44 (0)1349 830929
E-mail: *gomackay@btopenworld.com*

Introduction

This book is not purely autobiographical, and therefore not solely based on real events or persons. 'Kate', my 'mentor', for example, is an amalgam of several key influences on my personal journey to leadership.

My intent is to communicate practical truths of leadership based upon personal experience. By illustration, I provide examples that those leading or about to lead for the first time can relate to, and translate into their own areas of personal leadership activity.

Unlike many accounts of leadership I do emphasise that the path to leadership, as a journey, by no means begins on the day one is formally appointed as 'leader'. For any aspiring leader, the journey to authenticity necessitates the realisation of a degree of personal 'emotional intelligence' that cannot be gained from books or models. Its realisation constitutes a fundamental and unavoidable element in individual preparation for the trials and responsibilities of leadership.

The events described will be of most value to the aspiring leader if they are viewed as metaphors rather than an historical account. Occupying a region between fact and fiction, metaphors help us identify and focus upon recurrent 'patterns', of cause and effect, stimulating us to learn from them, just as we may do from the example of the Firebird's feather.

Beginning with an account of my personal unexpected induction into leadership the account then 'steps back' to examine prior events and my developing relationship with a mentor that was a precondition of my promotion. What then follows is a consideration of how, once appointed, I dealt with fear of failure, uncertainty and the personal responsibility for 'making things happen', where once I simply did as I was told by others.

Beyond this, each chapter is themed to consider a differing aspect of leadership in practice, drawing in no chronological order on my early days of leadership as informed by subsequent reflection.

Initiation: of mentors, meetings and missions (seemingly) impossible!

It was late October, just another rainy day in Edinburgh. The unexpected meeting, scheduled at short notice with company Director Kate Thompson, triggered no alarm bells. Walking to her office I felt no apprehension, no premonition; nevertheless, my world was about to be turned upside down.

Kate's call for a meeting was unexceptional in itself. Our paths crossed regularly in team meetings throughout the country, and so far as I was concerned, this was probably just another opportunity to 'touch base'.

In my mid-forties and now nearing completion of a four-year MBA by correspondence, I was a well-established IT consultant. But each week was much like another as I travelled between clients, attended meetings, wrote reports and so on.

Kate occupied a small office on her flying visits between sites across the UK and corporate headquarters in Paris. Seeing her there, I would never have guessed that within minutes she would catapult me into the greatest challenge and most rewarding adventure of my life to date.

Just a laptop computer, briefcase and a few documents lay on her desk. Inviting me in, and very much in character, without preamble or introduction she read out a recently received e-mail outlining a contract for us to set up and run a call centre for a large mobile-phone company.

It was a 3-month contract for 100 seats, occupied by trained staff, working shifts, to register details of the client's new customers. I remember at this point being slightly bemused; striving to comprehend what part I might play in the project. Where did I fit in? I had no significant operational or man-management experience, and virtually none in leadership. I knew little about the operation never mind the leadership of a call centre.

Yet, as Kate talked, like a breaking wave, comprehension flooded through me. The role she described was not for someone else but one she wanted *me* to take on!

I was, she said, to be Project Manager; to create and lead a team, transforming the top floor of the building into a fully functioning call centre, and then to manage it operationally as Call Centre Manager.

'Oh, and by the way', I remember her adding, as an afterthought, 'You'll need to recruit, select, and train 320 staff, covering multiple shifts over a 7-day week'!

My face must have been a picture, but then she added I had just 7 weeks until 7th December, when thousands of customer calls would come flooding in ...

I remember nothing we said in the minutes before I left Kate's office. I do remember being aware that I was at a turning point in my life. In the moment when Kate looked for my acceptance of the task before me, there might as well have been a 'flaming feather from the Firebird' flickering its challenge on the desk between us!

Standing outside her door, numb and awed, the magnitude of trust and responsibility laid upon me began to sink in. I felt something else stirring too; something deep, unexpected and, for me, quite profound.

In those first moments, although I was unsure where exactly to start my task, I felt that 'stirring' become an uncoiling of some, as yet undefined, new source of energy.

Personal success or the all-too-real fears of failure were as nothing compared with this motive force. I realised that my determination to succeed was now grounded in a single, crystallised steely conviction: 'I would not betray that trust. I would not let Kate down!'

Looking back, I realise this moment was a *cause* of all that followed, but importantly, it was also an *effect* of what went before. For anyone studying leadership in practice it is of value to consider how one becomes a leader and there are lessons to be learned from my own experience in this.

Standing outside Kate's office then, and now, years later, I recognise her pivotal role is reflected in classical mythology, for she bestowed upon me the mantle and challenge of leadership in a broader and more ancient context. She was now 'mentor', to me.

The notion of mentorship may be traced back to Homer's *Odyssey*, where the goddess Athena (goddess of wisdom!), in the guise of the old man Mentes, tutors and guides the son of Odysseus; Telemachus, who with Mentes as mentor, embarks on a quest to seek his 'lost' father and king. My relationship with Kate as 'mentor' was fundamental for it was this relationship that formed the basis on which she made the decision to empower me as leader.

People do not find themselves in positions of organisational leadership on a whim. Mine was not a name picked out of a hat but, importantly, neither was it on the basis of some demonstrated leadership competence. So what was the sequence of cause and effect that led to my selection for the role and what might others learn from this?

Getting there

Many months prior to the events described, I relaxed with several work colleagues in a Cambridge hotel bar. Among them was Kate; senior manager in another part of the company. We were seated, quite coincidentally it seemed, next to each other. We must have discussed a number of work-related projects but, by some unlikely twist of conversation, we discovered a shared and deep personal awareness of our dependency on, and sense of obligation to, our respective forbears.

Her father had laboured in the great steel mills of Sheffield, struggling from poor beginnings to set Kate's feet on a higher path. My father grew up on an isolated Hebridean island croft.

We both openly acknowledged our respective debt to their part in making us the best we could be. There was, I so vividly remember, a silent but emotionally charged moment our eyes met in some silent accord ...

In that moment we 'connected'; we established a 'platform of mutual trust and respect'. Be aware that there was no 'sexual chemistry' in this for either of us. I never saw Kate that way, and I had no desire to compromise our professional relationship.

Some weeks later I asked for a meeting with Kate. Fortuitously for me, her team had since expanded to include me, among others. Less fortuitously, as a result of other organisational changes, my own role had become rather limiting. I could not see any way forward or upwards. This, along with the stimulation of my MBA studies, left me feeling a need for greater challenge in my work.

During study for my MBA, I'd read numerous managerial case studies concerning strategy at senior levels within multi-national organisations. Doing so made me more aware than ever that I lacked any real experience of man management and leadership. I did not even really grasp the difference between the two functions. Certainly, I had practised some functional project management skills, leading meetings and groups in a limited way, but I had, as yet, little practical experience of day-to-day functional line management. I had never carried out a single performance review, never dealt with disciplinary or operational management issues, and never been 'solely' accountable for the success of any operation or project.

With all this in mind, and some vague sense she might be able to help, I asked to meet with Kate. I sought to set time aside specifically for this discussion which, I realised, was not one to have 'ad hoc' in a corridor or in passing. My memory of our previous conversation in Cambridge meant I felt no hesitation in turning to her for advice and guidance. On entering her office, as ever, she was disconcertingly direct, offering no comment on my desire for a change. 'So what is it you *do* want to do?' she asked.

Despite being un-nerved by this first experience of her professional directness, and her obviously expecting I would have thought this through already, I managed a semi-structured reply. I expressed my desire to develop the practical leadership skills necessary to complement the theoretical knowledge my MBA offered. I also remember vowing to myself to anticipate such questions from Kate in future. Kate made no promises, offered no comment as such, but she did undertake to take my aspirations into account if a suitable opportunity arose.

A notable quality at the heart of Kate's ability and credibility is something so low key it was all but invisible to me at that time. When Kate made that commitment, I knew she would hold to it ...

This meeting was the last time I saw Kate before that fateful day in Edinburgh previously described.

Kate's role and importance as mentor is clear. Until then I had always, naively, believed that to succeed and be 'promoted' I needed firstly to do a 'good job', and secondly to do well in interview for a better position. Reflecting upon my own initiation into leadership it was clear I had been mistaken, so what was going on?

I gave this much thought; how did my elevation to leadership occur in the absence of the formal processes I assumed almost invariably applied? I thought carefully about this and my experience in organisations big and small. I could not shake off the growing conviction that, underlying the formal process of selection, more fundamental dynamics are at work. At the same time I recognised that the process leading to my own 'initiation' into leadership is not a universal experience, but there do seem to be patterns and lessons to learn from.

Find your own best arena, gate-keeper, and mentor

Aspiring leaders will want to give themselves the best possible chance of being appointed to a position of leadership in a context where they are most likely to succeed. To do this it is therefore vital first to identify an 'arena' in which they are best suited to lead and then to ask: 'What kind of leadership context is right for me?' 'Would I feel comfortable surrounded by those who are male, female, younger, or older, more or less technical?'

Asking these questions, we may naturally tend to be thinking about leadership in our current line or place of work. But this may be a mistake. Simply seeking to become a leader 'wherever our circumstances find us now' may not present our best and unique 'arena' for future success, not least in leadership. So, in the event that the current place of work does not sit well with us how might we find such an arena?

Paradoxically, one way forward does *not* require us to focus upon an arena or context at all. If we can identify a person we respect enough to acknowledge willingly as a 'mentor', we automatically identify an appropriate arena in which to develop! Quite simply, in seeking and finding a potential mentor, someone we respect, who perceives 'what we are' and more importantly 'what we might become', we are likely to be drawn to a context where we will probably 'fit in'. It is not scientific but it can help us broaden our outlook to help identify arenas and paths to leadership outside our current workplace.

Rarely do we find the responsibilities and privileges of power bestowed on us unless 'someone', a specific person, bestows it, having recognised, at least in embryonic form, some latent capability for leadership within us.

In contemporary organisations, particularly large ones, the gate-keeping role of mentor may be obscured by formalised human resources-led selection and assessment/interview processes. Nevertheless, someone, a specific person, is usually responsible for making the final choice, and that choice is, perhaps more often than HR would wish us believe, based upon the subjective inclination of a single decision-maker.

Warning! The very moment we embark upon the process of identifying a mentor we simultaneously set in motion a potentially life-changing series of events. It is the moment we 'lift the Firebird's feather', and it is not a step to be taken lightly. Our 'mentor' will probably only be found in a context to which we are instinctively attracted. Therefore, seeking the gate-keeper we are simultaneously, though we may not realise it, seeking a path to realise our own true potential as a leader but also perhaps as a human being.

The difference between having an imposed teacher (or manager or leader) and having a 'mentor' is as fundamental as that between a true friend and a mere working acquaintance. If we aspire to leadership we therefore need to ask if there is anyone, where we are now, whether in work or in life in general, we respect enough to acknowledge willingly as our 'mentor'?

It may be uncomfortable, even painful, to acknowledge, but if we cannot identify a 'mentor' this raises an important question. If there is no 'mentor' on this path for us, then perhaps our being 'here' is not in our own long-term best interest?

Such considerations may not seem significant or 'practical' for everyone, of course. For many if not most, it may be enough to do a job, and go home with our earnings. For others, claims to 'immediate financial necessity' and job security may seem to preclude the 'luxury' of changing their environment, whether through changed employment, training or just changing where they live. But for every such claim of 'binding circumstance', there are and have always been 'exceptions': those who 'break free' and forge an alternative path to self-betterment.

I have recently, along with many others I am sure, been inspired by the successful endeavours of Dame Ellen Macarthur who, from a rural childhood in Derbyshire with no real links to the sailing world, has taken it by storm in her ascendance through the ranks, to become a living legend. Here is a grand example of someone following their instinct, against all apparent odds of background and opportunity.

In fact, reflecting upon all this, it may be difficult to find examples of 'great leaders' who have *not*, at some crucial point in their development, made exactly this sort of decision 'against the odds'. Again such situations evoke the image of that 'Firebird feather' upon the road.

Such people move on to embrace other and often strikingly different life-paths. Strangely, but not surprisingly, it is those who 'jump the tracks' who often go on to enjoy the most fulfilling careers, and, perhaps more importantly, lives. It is rare to meet folk regretting having consciously taken the 'path less travelled', far rarer than meeting those who mournfully, if not bitterly, claim 'they *could* have been a contender'!

First steps

We have now considered several factors leading to my standing outside Kate's office, having been set that '7-week challenge'. We have considered the centrality of the 'mentor' and some of the practical challenges facing those desiring entry into a leadership arena that is uniquely right for us, including the selection and interview process.

Standing outside Kate's office, I had already discovered a powerful ally in the battle to overcome any sense of personal inadequacy or fear of failure: my determination not to let her down.

My next and first steps were a 'leap into the unknown', but again a few simple insights gained from watching Kate in practice would serve me well, as I sought to navigate my way to establishing a plan, a team and, in just 7 weeks, a fully operational call centre.

3

Into the unknown: first steps in leadership

Certain questions Kate often used came to form the bedrock of my own leadership practice. As I left Kate's office on that fateful day, fortunately it was to these questions I was able to turn for guidance; their application helped me take those first steps into the unknown, and they still do today, as I face every new project and unfamiliar situation. They are so powerful not least because they help keep from my face the frozen expression characterised in cartoons of a rabbit caught in the headlights of an oncoming car or express train!

Facing the unknown as I assumed my new role as leader was not a one-off event for me or indeed any leader. Leadership is often about carrying out change, so every leader must, time and again, find ways to bridge the gap between how things are now and how they need to be in the future. It is about that moment when the path of the known runs out; when we face unfamiliar territory, and panic wells up inside; when we simply don't know what to do next. This feeling is very familiar on the path to leadership. Fortunately, simply experiencing this feeling reflects the fact that we are human, not that we are poor leaders. It is how we address the unknown rather than what we are 'feeling' that really matters. The questions I learned to ask whenever that 'grey wall of uncertainty' looms before me has meant that, as my experience grows, such moments become ever more fleeting.

I learned these questions initially simply by observing Kate's leadership of meetings, and I found myself increasingly turning to them whenever I found myself in situations where I was not sure how to proceed.

> I keep six honest serving-men
> (They taught me all I knew);
> Their names are What and Why and When
> And How and Where and Who. (Rudyard Kipling)

Kipling's honest serving-men open a door into greater understanding about where we are, want to be and how to get there. In a way the greatest gift a university education provides is the ability to frame questions using them. After all, for many graduates, the facts and figures taught on their courses are never subsequently used in 'real life'. Rather, what is absorbed, by those who apply themselves to their studies of even obscure subjects, is the ability to 'reason', and invariably this is simply about being able to frame intelligent questions using one or other of these simple words.

This became ever more apparent to me over the years, but in those early days when time and again I found myself in new and unfamiliar territory, I consistently deployed these four basic, quite specific questions. As you read and consider them, imagine you are me outside Kate's office that fateful day.

The four key questions

1. What are we trying to achieve (what does 'good' look like)?

OK, it *is* two questions, but the second merely clarifies the first! What is sought is a clear definition of the 'end' sought, in objective terms, as well as clear guidelines governing the way we get there. We must 'be specific'. Can we identify, in concrete terms, what will characterise success in our endeavour, what we are to achieve, and how? In meetings, for example, this question threw all previous discussion into sharp relief – were we 'on course', and aligned with the objective, or had we begun to 'drift'? It forced us to stop and think, to identify our objective(s) in concrete practical terms.

In the heat of any debate, many often diverse issues are thrown up. A contributor may raise points more to be seen as being important than for any merit in their argument. There may be positions adopted that simply reflect personalities or groups seeking to 'score points' against each other, rather than because of any adherence to arguments or positions in themselves. How often do debates degenerate into win/lose arguments having nothing to do with content and everything to do with personalities? As soon as we ask and demand a clear answer to the question of the specific 'ends' sought, it throws spurious arguments into sharp relief. How do we outline realistic objectives?

At this point it can be helpful to remember the mnemonic 'think SMART'. Our SMART objectives should be:

- *Specific* – again, be concrete. It's the difference between saying that customer service should be 'good' and saying that customer service should meet specific criteria that establish a level or standard that is

- *Measurable* – that can be objectively assessed and quantified. They should never be subjective and therefore dependent upon a specific individual's perception. This is the difference between qualitative and quantitative information. Quantitative information is objective.

- *Achievable* – this does not simply mean that objectives should 'seem' achievable, or that they are something we 'would like to think' is achievable. This step of definition is crucial, as any salesperson set unrealistic targets can testify. If targets are intended to motivate, then setting unrealistic targets is counter-productive. To make objectives achievable it is necessary to undertake research to establish what is actually achievable and this process in itself serves to highlight areas requiring attention. What are the bottlenecks restricting productivity? Do they come down to equipment, training, organisational structures or processes? Identifying what can be done to render objectives achievable can help us identify subsidiary actions that remove significant obstacles to enhanced performance.

■ *Realistic* – often confused or not sufficiently distinguished from 'achievable', a realistic objective takes account not so much of whether the end-point can be reached as what may prevent it. Climbing a mountain may be achievable under the right conditions but whether it is realistic may depend on 'who' is asked to climb, and when and how, etc. It is not so much about whether we can envisage the company or an individual 'being there', as whether we can envisage this particular person, group or company 'getting there'.

■ *Time-bound* – Murphy's Law that 'work expands to fill the time available' abides. It is vital that all objectives carry an 'expiry date'. Timescales and deadlines focus the mind wonderfully. Where sensible, as in all project management situations, we may end up with a string of linked activities each carrying a timescale with specific start and end dates as well as dependencies, reflecting the fact that one task must be complete before another can commence.

A vital benefit of asking what we are trying to achieve is that it forces us to envisage or visualise: to have a clear and now SMART 'vision' of where we want to be.

I have always found that once I strive to make my vision 'SMART', the path to that achievement begins to emerge as if by magic. 'I want to be able to fly' is a high aspiration, but there is an immense mental chasm between the aspiration and any possibility of its realisation. However, becoming 'specific', and realising that realistically we cannot (so far) physically sprout wings, leads us to recognise our need to meet two specific objectives: to get an aircraft of some description and gain the skills of a pilot.

These two clear objectives now serve to prompt further questions such as how and where etc. – each one making that bridge more real and tangible and, ultimately, crossable.

An integral part of this process of visualisation and concrete objective setting is crystallised by the next key question.

A year after setting up that first call centre I walked into a new call centre I was to take over for the first time; I knew almost nothing of the people who worked there, or the problems it, and they, suffered. I set myself a period of 2 weeks to do a lot of listening and asking questions. At the end of that period, in a meeting already referred to, I remember addressing a room full of managers and asking them how confident they were that I would get a meaningful answer if I asked any one of the agents or team leaders below them what characterised a 'good' agent or team leader? I still remember their looks, echoing various degrees of perplexity and even alarm. Immediately I knew that the call centre could *never* achieve success as long as the vast majority of people working there simply did not know 'what good looks like'!

SMART objectives pave the way to what we wish to achieve, whether in meetings where I first saw Kate deploy them, or in many other leadership contexts. But in addition to identifying 'where we are going', we must be clear about what is different about 'there', compared with 'here'? What will characterise our having arrived 'there', qualitatively and quantitatively? We must also understand what 'good looks like' in terms of the manner or 'way' in which we get there. Always, 'how' we work towards our objectives will influence, if not govern, what we ultimately achieve. So we must ask what 'good' looks like in terms of both the 'means' and the 'ends' we pursue.

These questions are so simple they are often not even asked – but they may well uncover factors that may otherwise remain obscured, implicit or even invisible (until it's too late!).

However, we must be careful that *our* perception of what good looks like also mirrors that of our client, whether our manager or a customer, and that those we lead share that perception or vision.

How often do we discover, after the event, that our perception of the problem to be solved or objective to achieve turned out in practice to be quite different from that of others or even ourselves?

Two things are involved here: making sure that our own perception is realistic, and that it is congruent and mirrors that of our stakeholders – bosses, clients and team. It is like standing at the base of a mountain and looking up at its distant peak. Declaring its attainment as our objective we set out to climb. Who, familiar with the mountains, has not experienced that sinking of the heart as a 'false summit' is reached? It was certainly the summit, as seen from the ground, but there, along a ridge or across an intervening descent, the true summit soars yet higher above us.

As a leader it is vital we distinguish between the 'presenting' problem, or the 'apparent' objective, and the real one, and that as this perception often changes over time it is shared with all stakeholders.

Does the manner in which the objectives are presented imply, govern, influence or even demand how they are to be achieved? When set objectives, we must carefully ensure our perception of what constitutes success reflects that of the person setting the task. We do not want to reach what we thought was the objective to find this 'is not quite' what was sought, by whoever set the task.

Imagine you are tasked with 'improving the organisation'. This might traditionally be achieved by tightening up finance, or improvements in the machinery, technology, communications networks, systems, etc. It might also be achieved by enhancing morale so that fewer people leave, and encouraging better communication to increase efficiency. Both approaches are very different, but both clearly achieve the objective as stated.

It is a simple example. But if we seek to identify and clarify assumptions, look behind 'presented' problems or objectives', we will often discover what our objectives *really* are.

Building and communicating a clear picture of where we want to be, and what will define success in quantifiable objective terms, also helps keep a meeting or project team aligned and focused on the same ends: 'singing from the same hymn-sheet'.

Agreeing a shared vision of what is to be achieved with each stakeholder is crucial, but it does not necessarily tell us *how* to get there and, as a leader, we must be able to inspire a team to appreciate how doing what may be onerous (or, in extreme situations, dangerous) is meaningful for them.

This may require us to invest the mundane or boring, unpleasant or downright dangerous with a 'spark of significance', to which they can relate. Imagine a visitor being shown around a quarry where, when asked, one mason with slumping shoulders replies he is simply cutting stone, while another proudly jumps to his feet and makes a sweeping gesture of his hand and points grandly to a mighty cathedral saying, 'I'm building that'!

Same job, but vastly different perceptions and attitudes. It is not difficult to imagine the quality of work by these two masons resulting from such contrasting perceptions and attitudes. This emphasises another key lesson. If people can see what is asked of them as being genuinely significant, in terms that are individually meaningful to them, then their willing and enthusiastic engagement with the task is far more likely. This becomes all the more important in contemporary industry, where the worker rarely sees the final product of their labours.

So, setting a SMART vision and inspiring the team achieves little in and of itself, if the way between 'here' and 'there' is not made clear and objectives are not shared and congruent. So far we have identified where we want to be, and something about the manner of getting there. Unfortunately, very often when objectives are set another vital consideration can be missed.

2. Where are we now?

A call centre I was asked to take over at very short notice was in breach of contract with the client, owing to its poor quality of service. I only had a couple of hours of briefing with the outgoing manager before I was on my own. Another wall of uncertainty loomed before me. But I applied the first question, and to some extent all was well. This second question, however, revealed the source of many problems. The presence of any organisational function of MIS or Management Information Service was noticeable largely by its almost total absence. As a result it was little wonder that objectives were not being realised. How could weaknesses or areas for focus be addressed if they were all but invisible?

High on my list of priorities was to establish an MIS function that provided relevant Key Performance Indicators (KPIs) reflecting the client's Service Level Agreement (SLA). Soon, and for the first time, the call centre and everyone in it knew 'where they were', in relation to 'where they needed to be'. Progress was as swift as it was certain.

To define where we are now, we should employ exactly the same measures used to define our end-point. So, if we are seeking to achieve a set measure of mechanical, systemic or technical efficiency, or a particular measure of customer satisfaction, we need to quantify what it is now. If we do not, how can we measure progress away from where we are, never mind towards the objective.

When asking 'where are we now' it can also be revealing to ask 'why' and 'how' we came to be here.

Taking over that call centre these questions revealed that one reason for poor performance arose from the low morale of the staff, which led to high turnover ('churn' as it is known in the call centre industry). The job advertisement to which they had responded offered 'jobs to fit your lifestyle'. It is not surprising that morale slumped, and the local press became involved when, after training, mothers with children for example were *told* the shifts they would be working. We will return to this example in Chapter 4, but understanding where we were, and why, soon dissolved any uncertainty about an issue that clearly had to be addressed. To appreciate the importance of this question, imagine my focus had solely turned on 'setting objectives', and 'what good looks like', in the absence of any consideration as to the reality on the ground, and what made things the way they were? One analogy for this is that not checking where we are, and what lies, behind, is like jumping into a car and pulling out with no regard for what is going on around, or for that juggernaut thundering up behind us.

Focusing ahead, on objectives, is vital, but so is the importance of 'where we are now', including our gaining some understanding of the legacy we inherit that, if we are not forewarned, may creep up from behind as we focus far ahead on the blue horizon.

3. How to we get from here to there?

By now the grey wall of uncertainty had well and truly begun to dissolve. Applying the preceding questions I was well on the way to clarity about how to go about setting up a call centre in 7 weeks. Simply asking the first 'what am I trying to achieve?' led to my seeking specific information about the nature of the service required and the SLA I would have to meet, and led to my learning from both client and employer their views on how this was to be achieved. Like any explorer I now had before me a kind of map. I had learned by asking 'where I was' – how and why the contract had been given to my company – the terrain behind was understood, and an agreed objective had been quantified. I had accumulated key information that informed and even prompted all my subsequent planning.

Standing outside Kate's office I was of course able to answer the first question for myself relatively quickly compared with the subsequent situation in which I inherited leadership of an existing call centre. In terms of where we were, I knew I was breaking new ground, as my company had never set up a call centre before, so there was little by way of inheritance or legacy issues I needed to worry about. The good news was that my company did have a number of project management tools and policies and simply discovering the inputs they needed set me well on the way to establishing my first project plan.

My first task on getting to my desk, however, was to sketch out the simplest of project plans without computers or any other guidance. I just set about listing everything I could imagine we might need, not least of which was the requisite skill-sets, and corresponding internal teams I would need input from. One valuable lesson learnt in those first 24 hours was that it would have been very easy to fail entirely, had I overlooked one key link in the chain. Thinking about the project as a whole, a 'helicopter view' if you like, I realised that a fundamental requirement would be the establishment of a high-volume data-link between ourselves in Edinburgh and the client's computers in Bristol.

I phoned the telecommunications provider used by our company to discover that they had a 45-day lead time for installation: just less than 7 weeks! This shows the value, at an early stage, of ensuring, where 'outside' contractors or suppliers are involved, that delivery can be assured within the requirements of the project. Fortunately everything else could be put in place before the line was installed, although it did rather curtail the available on-line training that would be possible and our training had to take due account of this.

Project planning

In every sphere of leadership it is likely that to a greater or lesser extent there will be real value in establishing a formal structured project plan, and for this reason some general guidelines and lessons learnt in this area are offered.

A project plan, whether on a sheet of paper for a small project or using a more or less sophisticated software package, will identify the project's 'milestones', a 'critical path' and relevant 'dependencies'. The critical path reflects dependencies, ensuring that everything occurs in proper sequence; we do not want the electrician turning up when the walls have already been plastered and papered!

In order to structure a project of any significant size, I learned that four factors are key. Note that they can in fact be applied to almost *any* objective we or others are set:

- *Performance*. This will reflect our definition of 'what good looks like'. What constitutes good performance? There are often compromises to be made – quality can be expensive; do we need a Ferrari or a truck?

- *Cost*. How much can we spend, and how fixed is that amount? Can the scope of the project or the time taken be altered to work within the cost?

- *Timescales*. How much time is available to do the task? Can it be altered or reduced by addressing cost, scope or performance?

- *Scope*. What does the task include and importantly what is *not* our responsibility? For example, in setting up the call centre I did not need to worry about security or general building maintenance.

Having quantified each of these factors it is usually recommended that the project manager ensures that they have flexibility on at least one parameter. To proceed otherwise is to risk failure to deliver.

The longer the lifetime of the project the more this holds true. In any project an inevitable degree of unforeseeable change and uncertainty creeps in over time. These unforeseen factors can descend on us from any direction: time available, or taken, materials or labour, all may suffer from increases in cost due to inflation/deflation/availability, none of which may appear to be a likely issue when the project is initiated.

Perception management

Good project managers are keenly aware that without customer perception management they may be presumed to have failed because, for any number of reasons, measures of success become focused on one area, despite all others being on target. It is therefore vital to understand from the outset how success will be measured – what are the priorities – 'what does good look like'? Warning: driven by politics or other considerations these priorities, too, can change over time, and the astute project manager ensures they remain as far as possible in touch with such trends. Ultimately the best guarantee is to ensure that objectives and priorities are clearly defined, written up and agreed by the client, together with any changes along the way.

From the preceding emerges the value of my final key question. This addresses the dynamic nature of organisational life. Over the period between objective setting and its accomplishment, things will change, whether they are priorities or the environmental context.

The captain of a sailing ship or a pilot plotting a course from one port or airport to another sets out with a clear objective in mind, taking due account of the known prevailing wind direction, magnetic deviation and other factors, to arrive at a bearing on which to sail the ship or fly the aircraft. Once en route, however, unforeseeable factors invariably come into play. Among these may be changes regarding their craft or the ever changing environment. At regular intervals, the captain and pilot seek landmarks previously highlighted on their charts to establish if they are drifting off track. At this point a change in course may be called for to make up for any error-to-date, and to anticipate its ongoing effect throughout the duration of the journey. Particularly adverse weather may require a fundamental change of plan or a 'diversion' to some planned-for alternative destination.

Similar challenges to these face the leader seeking achievement of their objectives, whether organisational or personal.

For this reason, at regular intervals, key questions 1–3 should be regularly qualified in the light of the fourth.

4. What has changed?

The kind of changes to be identified may emerge in diverse areas:

- The 'environment', however defined:
  - micro-organisational (changes in subordinate team, organisational structures and processes?)
  - competition (what are they doing?)
  - sociological (are practices or products becoming less politically correct or acceptable?)
  - technological (is emerging technology rendering current practices, products, etc., obsolete?)
  - economic (are projected and actual profitability aligned? Is the economic market or demand changing? Why?)
  - political (with large and small 'p': are changes significant?). The STEP analysis was developed by Fahey and Narayanan in their book *Macro Environmental Analysis for Strategic Management*.
- Personal objectives and priorities (has anything changed to necessitate their re-evaluation?)
- Macro-organisational (changed leadership, broader organisational focus, direction/strategy, etc.)

What emerges is a cycle of questions the leader can and should deploy, to considerable advantage, in *any* organisational context.

With time and practice, the leader will find themselves benefiting from what others may perceive to be an 'uncanny knack' or instinct for being ever-alert to what is 'significant' in any given situation, in much the same way that our aforementioned sailor or pilot, through many patient hours of structured instrument scanning, or observing sails and weather, finds their eye unerringly drawn to that one sail or gauge telling them that something significant has or is changing!

This mental skill is often referred to as a 'motor skill'. Just as the learner cyclist, driver, musician, skier, footballer, etc., must spend patient hours mechanically 'going through the motions' until such skills become second nature, so too the accomplished leader will have nurtured and developed their own skills through the classic process of competence development:

From

- unconscious incompetence – doing it badly and not even realising it,

  to

- conscious incompetence – doing it badly and knowing it,

  to

- conscious competence – doing it right but mechanically,

  to

- unconscious competence – doing it right instinctively – even transcending the 'rules'; like an accomplished jazz musician etc.

The application of the techniques and the 'key questions' described are not purely applicable to project management, however. As I began my project to set up a call centre in

7 weeks, I successfully applied them time and again, whether in the micro-environment of a meeting, setting and tracking personal objectives, or in relation to organisation-wide issues. In the case of the latter, for example, they informed my thinking as I considered where we were, and what needed to be done in order to meet project deadlines. I used them in the previously mentioned 'turn-round' of a new call centre already in breach of contract. I was able to lead that call centre from being 'worst of thirteen', to 'number one' in 3 months as measured by an external company's audit of our performance, largely as a result of asking the right questions at the outset.

Note

The deployment of these 'four questions' can inform the leader at *every* turn in organisational life, whatever the context. They apply over and over again, in every area of leadership this book addresses; the reader is encouraged to consider and seek to apply them until the process becomes automatic. In time the questions themselves become second nature as one becomes 'unconsciously competent'.

Preparing for the path of leadership

As my own case shows, the path to leadership begins long before our formal appointment to a leadership position. Looking back over my own experience and considering the examples of others it is possible to identify specific competences that may be developed to great advantage when the mantle of leadership is assumed for the first time.

In the text that follows the aspiring leader is encouraged through the development of reflexivity and self-leadership to evaluate their own personal strengths and weaknesses, and to test their motives thoroughly before they are put to the test in the crucible of practice, where the absence of such preparation has proved devastating for both leaders and those who follow.

The power of reflexivity

In the Prologue I mentioned that I learned much about the nature and practice of leadership by reflecting upon my own experience of being led. It is readily overlooked, but in itself this statement reflects the operation of a core if not *the* core competence of all good leaders: reflexivity.

One may well discover, however, that too overt a practice of reflexivity is not broadly welcomed in many organisational environments. My first conscious awareness of this came shortly after I left the Royal Navy.

At the time I was attending university as a mature student when I came across the phrase 'trained incapacity'. I was researching an article for a magazine where I covered, among other things, the manner in which the military and other organisations proscribe and limit certain competencies and faculties.

My 5½-year Royal Naval engineering apprenticeship taught me to fix, maintain and operate a wide range of engines, boilers and other equipment, at sea. These analytical and reflective skills when purely focused upon an engineering task were seen as well and good, but this ability critically to assess, analyse and diagnose were never going to be so welcome if applied by a subordinate critically to assess their own officers' competence!

'Insubordination' is simply refusing overtly to be subordinate. Clearly it is not a good idea, especially in the military, to have everyone questioning and second guessing their leadership. Unquestioning obedience, compliance and deference to officers greatly facilitates the smooth, rapid, concerted operation of large-scale military manoeuvres.

Some specialised exceptions to this mode of leadership (although strictly it's more 'coercion' than 'leadership') exist in the military such as that found in the British SAS (Special Air Service). There, an officer's decision-making is, wherever practicable, open to question and suggestion in what they call a 'Chinese Parliament'. But once the officer's decision is made, it is expected to be unquestioningly adhered to by all. The pride and loyalty found in the SAS are legendary and something I learned from this is that gaining 'buy-in' from team members really does secure far greater commitment and engagement in securing objectives than coercion.

'Unquestioning' compliance and the establishment of 'trained incapacity' undoubtedly makes leadership less challenging in the sense that decisions are not open for discussion. Anyone who has been led under such conditions knows how limiting this can be, however. 'Trained incapacity' arises when the organisation seeks to circumscribe and limit our ability to think for ourselves, to set a boundary upon what we may question. This encourages the individual to be lazy as they let others do the thinking for them, and applies as much to an employee, housewife or henpecked husband as it does to the soldier or sailor under military rule.

Once I became alerted to the existence and idea of trained incapacity, it seemed to crop up in every facet of my life. I remember, for example, an open-air event following which, sitting in a coach, I heard the radio announce in 'measured authoritative tones' that 'the last of those attending the event departed some time ago'. Yet outside I could clearly see thousands of people still making their way home. Ever since then I have been keenly aware that news presented by the media is rarely as objective as those 'selling it' would have us believe. Reflexivity is about learning to ask questions, perhaps especially when encouraged not to do so.

For any leader, a healthy dose of scepticism and questioning about 'the facts as presented' is good practice. A gullible leader is easy prey for misinformation and manipulation by others. The aspiring leader recognises that trained incapacity encourages an approach to organisational and personal life that is the diametric opposite of reflexivity.

Reflexivity also helps us bear with the discomfort of being led poorly, as it provides the relief of a broader perspective. We will not always labour under a poor leader; we can turn even bad experiences to our own and eventually others' benefit.

With reflexivity we regularly 'take stock'. The four questions can help in this as they help broaden our perspective; we 'rise above the trees' in our mind's eye to 'see the wood'.

It is a powerful mental tool that facilitates our escape from the insidious tendencies of trained incapacity.

Management and leadership studies taught me a tool I found particularly helpful in my developing personal practice of reflexivity. It is called the 'Johari window', and provides a vivid illustration of the potential divorce between personal reality and the world around us. The version presented on p.32 encourages us to reflect upon and thereby begin to inform the 'hidden self': aspects of our personality, abilities and our perceptions of them that may be at odds with those around us. If we can do this through honest reflection it can prove an invaluable aid to ensure our self-perception does not diverge unacceptably far from organisational (and even domestic) reality.

The Johari window

Us as we *see* ourselves	Us as we *think* others see us
The hidden self	Us as others *actually* see us

Imagine you are given a sheet of paper and are asked to list 20 things that describe you: what you are good and bad at, your likes and dislikes, your best friends, your aspirations, etc. This is what informs the top left corner of the window. Now imagine you are given a number of sheets and are asked to list the same defining characteristics, but this time each sheet reflects how we *think* others see us (family members, friends, work colleagues or our boss, for example). Finally, imagine that each individual you identified were independently approached and asked to give their *actual* views on us. How uncomfortable might the emerging differences be?

A vivid example is drawn if one imagines David Brent in the award-winning TV series *The Office* considering himself as 'able and admired', despite the rather different perceptions reflected by those around him.

Asking questions *that* the Johari window prompts, about how we see and seem to others, highlights sometimes uncomfortable, often surprising, even disturbing differences in perception. If we can identify areas of 'discomfort', where we are 'not sure' whether our perception is accurate, then we have at least a starting point to find ways to explore these differences.

A competent leader sees themselves as others see them, and so recognises how the way they speak or present themselves affects others. I recently observed a leader approach an older person of the opposite sex. They stood over them such that the person they were 'commanding' had to strain their neck to look up over their shoulder. They could not even move back to a more comfortable position because the leader had effectively crowded them against their desk. It was perfectly clear to me this approach was not likely to win the leader involved much by way of support! I suspect that if they could have seen a video of this encounter they would likely have cringed. As a leader we should be running that 'video' constantly to see ourselves as we are seen.

As a competent leader we should also seek to encourage reflexivity in others. I encouraged reflexivity in my managers by asking them, in private one-to-one conversations, what they thought their team members would say if I asked about their manager's strengths and weaknesses. This often also served to prompt them to identify and volunteer insights it would have been difficult for me to raise directly, without appearing confrontational.

360 degree feedback

360 degree feedback has enjoyed vogue in some organisational settings and is often advocated in academic, management and human resources literature. But for many the idea of opening oneself up to potential 'bad news and negative views' from those led or managed is not welcome.

It is not difficult to see or appreciate why this should be so. It is an invariable fact of life that one cannot be liked by all the people all the time, and in any case, many would argue, 'it's not my job to be "liked" but to get things done' or 'I don't expect you to "like" me, just do what you are told!'

It is certainly clear that 360 degree feedback offers considerable potential for abuse. In my own experience I have known an organisation to manipulate review outcomes by employing 'leading questions' intended to suppress the positive whilst emphasising the negative and vice versa.

Equally, in theory, the leader and manager might gain significantly from 360 degree feedback if it is open, honest and carries no taint of vindictiveness. Paradoxically, it subverts 'trained incapacity' by encouraging upward questioning and criticism. For this reason it is rare to find the practice embraced in organisational contexts where unquestioning obedience is encouraged, or deemed necessary.

Traditional leaders' discomfited views on 360 degree feedback may also be voiced in terms asking: 'What can a technician tell *me* about management or leadership? They should stick to there own area of expertise; do their own job, and let me do mine!' The difficulty lies in sorting genuinely useful insights and views from those influenced by any number of personal, inter-personal or organisational factors.

Few do not hold some more-or-less informed view on how well or badly they are led and managed. For many, their response will be informed by their own social and organisational position, not least what views 'they think' others will expect them to espouse: the unique 'politics' of their social and organisational situation.

Ultimately, therefore, although there should be real value in 'objective' 360 degree feedback, the difficulties in realising it are significant. But for the aspiring leader, a nurtured ability to perceive one's effect on others, to measure and weigh one's approach to individuals and groups with the end to be achieved clearly in mind, is a must. This, too, is a clear competence, and while some may be 'gifted' to a greater or lesser degree it can be nurtured in most.

In effect, the practice of reflexivity in itself constitutes a 'virtual' 360 degree feedback function. Its effectiveness is of course limited by the acuteness of our perception of others as well as our ability to be honest with ourselves. Ultimately, however, a clear benefit of this approach is that it can be somewhat easier to assess if we are being honest with ourselves than to second guess whether others are being honest with us and themselves.

Developing reflexivity as a personal leadership competence by observing the leadership of others, we should ask what we would do in their stead. How we are led may not make us feel very 'happy' sometimes, but we do well to remember that 'happiness' and such transient feelings are not what competent leadership is about. The leader's function is invariably one in which occasionally unpopular decisions must inevitably be taken. The good of the many or the organisation will often come at the expense of the happiness of someone, or many, somewhere or other. Observing the leadership of others we should be asking questions as to their effectiveness. Sometimes it is indeed better to facilitate 'happiness', to encourage the team, but equally, at other times, nothing but 'blood sweat and tears' will in fact get the job done.

Reflexivity can be brought to bear in assessing and learning from the leadership of our own practice too. It can also help us understand what motivates others.

I remember vividly an early meeting I held with a group of unfamiliar operations managers in the call centre where I had been asked to 'turn-around' performance. In this first meeting I found myself setting an expectation that clearly came as something of a surprise to those present – not least me; I was often amazed at the sudden emergence and crystallisation of ideas when 'on the hoof' and under pressure.

I made it clear that within a few weeks I expected to be able to ask any operations manager to sketch out for me the aspirations, motivations, aversions, strengths and weaknesses in performance of each member of the team leaders in their charge. I also expected them in turn to set this requirement with each of their respective team leaders.

The initial reactions of discomfort I perceived to this objective undoubtedly arose because for most the notion of leadership is simply about 'telling others what to do': 'putting out' rather than 'taking in'. Nothing could be further from the truth. In reality the competent leader achieves results from 'the way' they set about this, and the 'way' should always be informed by a sound knowledge of the team as a whole and its members. The skills of inspirational oratory are infrequently applicable in the workplace and the slog of day-to-day long-term leadership necessitates due account being taken, so far as is practicable, of the motivations of the team and the individuals that constitute it.

Of the path of leadership itself; what does good look like?

Where did our personal conception of what good leadership is come from? Does it turn on results or how they are achieved?

Why do so few books on leadership address this? The danger inherent of not addressing it is that if we aspire to and head off along the road to leadership, without first understanding the origin of our own motivation and aspiration, then we are headed for real trouble when the clouds lower, the storms rise, masts break, power fails and the lights go out.

As with any project we face as a leader it is therefore a good idea to ask early 'what good looks like', 'where are we now' and 'how we get there'.

A priest described to me how, following the death of his father, he had gone home as Executor of the Will to find himself sitting at the very desk where, long before ordination, he sat to study theology. Sitting alone, in a priest's cassock, he was surprised to catch himself imagining his mother, who died some time before, standing and smiling over her son, 'the priest'. Suddenly he was surprised to be almost overwhelmed by a sudden surge of anger as he realised for the first time that he had become a priest simply to please her, to make her proud of him.

Undoubtedly, his motivation and sense of direction were strong when first he took the long road to priesthood, but only now, years later, was he moved really to question them. Some months later I heard he left the priesthood, was happily engaged in a fulfilling relationship and was working abroad teaching English.

As with the vocation of priesthood, the road to leadership is not to be taken lightly. The lives of others will be significantly affected by their leaders, in whatever sphere, and although rarely in such extreme conditions as the famous leaders we read about, we all must expect genuine crises to arise. Such is not the best time to find oneself considering how and why one got to be there in the first place.

Consider the example set by Sir Ernest Shackleton in 1915. As expedition leader his primary goal was to reach the South Pole. In this, he singularly failed. His ship, the *Endurance*, set sail for Antarctica, became ice-bound, then sank, leaving him and his men stranded on the ice. At this point, had Shackleton no clear convictions about the nature of his own leadership and role, then his personal sense of failure at this point might well have been overwhelming.

Undeterred, he knew success or failure in terms of the primary objective fell second to his role as a leader. He now consciously changed his goal to that dictated by circumstances: to getting all his men home, alive. No 'railing against the fates'; he saw what needed to be done and got on with it. The bald facts of the expedition are as follows.

Shackleton's journey

- 26th October 1914: leaves Buenos Aires.
- 5th December 1914: leaves South Georgia (last time crew would touch land for 497 days).
- 18th January 1915: ice-bound.
- 1st May 1915: sun sets, not rising for 4 months.
- 27th October 1915: abandons foundering *Endurance*.
- 21st November 1915: *Endurance* sinks.
- 9th April 1916: into lifeboats.
- 16th April 1916: reaches Elephant Island (first landfall in 15 months).
- 24th April 1915: leaves in open lifeboat *James Caird* (22′ long 6′6″ beam).
- 10th May 1916: landfall after 650 miles on South Georgia.
- 19th May 1916: sets out over unmapped mountains to Whaling Station at Husvik.
- 20th May 1916: reaches Stromness Whaling Station.
- All 27 members of the crew were rescued, and reached home.

Acknowledgement: *http://www.pbs.org/wgbh/nova/ shackleton/1914/timeline.html*

Shackleton's achievement in the face of overwhelming adversity was staggering. Reading the account now, in an age where mobile phones and satellite navigation are readily available to the general public, it is hard to comprehend that, after leaving South Georgia, neither Shackleton nor the rest of the crew saw or were in any contact with the outside world until 16 months later.

Imagine Shackleton's prospects as he and his men stood, alone on the ice, with only such provisions as they could rescue from the foundering ship, and a few small open lifeboats to get them home. No radio, no telephone and no satellite navigation. Imagine the all-pervading cold, the relatively primitive clothing and footwear, and the dwindling provisions. Imagine the strength of spirit necessary to maintain not only your own but the spirits of all the other men. Then we can gain a glimpse of what led Sir Raymond Priestley, a member of the 1907–09 Nimrod Expedition, to say:

> For scientific leadership give me Scott,
> For swift and efficient travel give me Amundsen.
> But when you are in a hopeless situation,
> When you are seeing no way out,
> Get down on your knees and pray for Shackleton.

Justifiably, Shackleton received many accolades for his achievements, but interestingly, the perceived 'failure' of his expedition, compared with those of Scott, was such that the magnitude of his leadership qualities were never fully acknowledged in his own lifetime. Sometimes leadership is purely measured in terms of success or failure, in reaching organisational objectives alone. Again, if the leader is not to be crushed by such judgements of their leadership they must be very clear in their own minds 'what they are about', and why.

For Shackleton, one of the greatest accolades followed shortly after his return. On a whaling ship anchored off South Georgia, one by one, hardened Norwegian whalers – veteran sailors of the harshest seas in the world – came forward to shake his hand in recognition of his leadership on a voyage in a small open boat over 650 miles from Elephant Island to South Georgia, through gale and hurricane. Just a few degrees off course, and they would have missed the island altogether. Shackleton relished the praise of those who 'knew' and were truly his peers, over all subsequent praise or judgement in the outside world.

The story and example of Shackleton is in every sense inspiring when it comes to illustrating pure leadership. As we have seen, much can be learned by the aspiring leader who reflects upon it even today, nearly a hundred years later.

It is clear that the leader in any sphere may be confronted by situations beyond anything imagined or considered when they took the job. Little wonder Shackleton's newspaper advert for the expedition read as follows:

> Men wanted: For hazardous journey. Small wages, bitter cold, long months of complete darkness, constant danger, safe return doubtful. Honour and recognition in case of success. (Sir Ernest Shackleton)

For this reason it is vital to understand why we are doing what we do; why it matters to us. This will also, incidentally, give us a sense of self-assurance that communicates itself to others.

Loneliness and the leader

'It is lonely; leadership'. I remember someone I had mentored saying this to me, after assuming his own leadership of a call centre. He explained he had never appreciated *just* how lonely it was to be a leader. There is always a 'distance' that cannot be closed between the leader and the led.

This is something I was surprised to discover is often required by the led as much as it is needed by the leader. However, in this loneliness great comfort and inspiration may be found in the accounts of other leaders. Let's face it, few of us are ever going to be called upon to demonstrate the qualities required of Shackleton, and his example is a beacon – if he could find the energy and strength to lead at the 'ends of the Earth' in such circumstances, then we may take comfort in his example. It can be done, no matter how low and dispirited we may feel, no matter the odds; where there is life, there truly is hope!

'For sudden, worst turns the best to the brave'. These words, quoted from Shakespeare's *Henry V* by Shackleton to his men on the Antarctic ice, reflect his ability to transcend even the most hopeless situation, turning it into a springboard for ever greater achievement.

A. H. Macklin, in 'Shackleton as I Knew Him', an unpublished manuscript quoted in the comprehensive biography *Shackleton* by Roland Huntford, described such a moment eloquently:

> It must have been a moment of bitter disappointment to Shackleton – he had lost his ship, and with her any chance of crossing the Antarctic Continent, but he showed it in neither word or manner. As always with

him what had happened had happened; it was in the past and he looked to the future ... without emotion, melodrama or excitement [he] said 'ship and stores have gone – so now we'll go home' – I think it would be difficult to convey just what those words meant to us, situated as we were, surrounded by jostling ice floes as far as the eye could reach, tired out with our efforts to save the ship, and with no idea as to what was likely to happen to us – 'We'll go home'.

Examples of great leaders often inspired me when the going got tough, and informed me about 'what good looks like' in a leader. There are of course many bad examples of leadership I experienced that lingered in my memory; leaders who left me feeling belittled or small. But as with Shackleton's 'worst to the brave' I make a conscious point of not erasing such experiences from my memory. Practising reflexivity I learned much from even the worst of experiences. Dag Hammarskjöld, ex Secretary General of the United Nations, said:

Your position never gives you the right to command. It only imposes on you the duty of so living your life that others can receive your orders without being humiliated.

What this taught me is *not* about my not giving others humiliating tasks; circumstances may require that. Shackleton had all his officers, including himself, assigned domestic duties on board the *Endurance*. The humiliation Hammarskjöld refers to is that which arises when we perceive our leader as weak, or one we are ashamed to acknowledge the organisation or world deems in some way our 'better'. As a leader I am therefore always conscious that for others to look to me as a leader I must represent myself in a way that will not compromise their sense of what a good leader looks like – as well as my own!

Being a leader is as much about what we are and how we are perceived as being about what we 'do'. Obviously what we do, or achieve, impacts how others see us, either positively or negatively, but beneath that, it is the kind of person we are that attracts or repels loyalty.

In this chapter we have considered how reflexivity and self-leadership can help us prepare for and walk the path of leadership. We have identified the self-knowledge and self-discipline leaders should seek to develop before the responsibilities of leadership are taken on. They need the self-assurance and conviction that comes from being quite clear about why you 'took the job', and the danger of doing so because of others' 'expectations of you'.

Reflexivity also prompts us to take account of those we lead, to consider the impact our words or actions are having upon them. Are we sending out the right signals? Are some things better left unsaid? Leadership credibility often turns on how we are perceived as individuals, and if we are to transmit these qualities then we must learn to be keenly conscious of the effect we are having on others. This is something that might be 'faked', but only in the short term. As with many qualities of leadership, this is a challenge and can be quite intimidating. 'I am not worthy' is a feeling most have had at one time or another. This is especially true in adversity, and no doubt Shackleton, Ellen Macarthur and every captain of industry knows moments of self-doubt. What often 'saw them through' though was a conviction that they would not let themselves, or those who looked up to them, down.

Authentic leadership

Authenticity is not simply a matter of 'putting on an act' but rather is about learning to find and release our often hidden or latent competences. It is about learning to draw upon and encourage our better qualities. The development of personal techniques to transcend our transient 'feelings of the moment' (emotional maturity) leads to credible and authentic leadership. Reflexivity is central in this process. When we and those around us feel down or discouraged, it is the leader who seeks and finds ways to transcend immediate problems – to see the big picture and the benefits attending achievement of our objectives. But if we are to do this for others, we must first learn mastery over our own transient emotions.

Leaders are as much responsible for informing the perceptions and feelings of the team about the challenges faced as they are for navigating their way through them. The cold numbed fingers, clinging to icy sails and beams far above a heaving deck, are an extension of the captain's leadership; if the commitment of the person behind them lacks resolve or understanding, this too is a measure of failed leadership.

4

Turning a crowd into a team

A crew or team may become more than the sum of its parts and this calls for the generation of a phenomenon known as 'synergy'. Synergy is present in the qualities that appear over and above its individual parts, just as an assembled car or aircraft is more than its individual components: the ability to travel, fly, etc. Where people are concerned, whether they play on the football field or work in a corporate organisation, synergy may also represent the difference between success and failure.

The creation of a team can occur under the pressure of an externally imposed threat, or by internally generated leadership, or some combination of both. As any football manager or coach would readily agree though, a team is not built by focusing purely on the performance of the team as a whole. It is not sufficient to urge a group of people to 'work as a team'. Rather, the successful leader takes into account each member of the team as an individual, as well as their performance as a group.

The teams I led in setting up and running call centres differed in fundamental ways. Set-up teams consisted of technical experts whose knowledge far exceeded mine in their various spheres, and I was largely limited in my choice by who was available for the project. Those who would run the call centre, by contrast, would be interviewed and selected and, in the case of the Operations Managers, this process would require my direct involvement.

As might be imagined, I was intensely conscious, in leading the former group, that there was a very real challenge facing me in establishing and following our project plan. The people I was asking for information regarding the resources and time necessary to any one task knew that I knew far less than them. I therefore realised that I would somehow need to convince them, at an early stage for example, that they could not mislead me into thinking that a task would take longer than necessary.

I was fortunate, however, that in such a large organisation, with which I was by then quite familiar, I was able to draw upon a number of technical experts outside my immediate team. From them I was able to gain some few key insights into what was involved for any given task and this meant I could communicate a credible understanding of the nature of each task. If a timescale or reasons for it not being achieved was offered I might defer responding there and then but would verify its being a credible excuse from another 'expert'. On other occasions I would quite explicitly ask what a team member thought 'X' might say if asked ... I learned, somewhat to my surprise at the time, that you really do not need to know the detail of the jobs of those you lead. You are there to lead and facilitate and, as such, in addition to co-ordinating, some time and thought simply needs to be given to gauging how the ongoing capability, focus and honesty of the team can be verified.

Another technique I employed in this regard was to ensure within each project team meeting that I made a point of establishing eye contact with each team member, explicitly asking what problems might arise before the next meeting or milestone. If there were issues, I asked what *they* were going to do about them, but if they were able with confidence to say that everything was in good shape, I knew they were going to be conscious that egg would be on *their* faces (as much as mine) if they subsequently reported failure. This tactic achieved real buy-in – ensuring each team member had a vested interest in achieving our objectives.

In such a technical project team I found, as leader, that the individuals share quite contrasting personality characteristics to those such as call-centre staff in a 'people-orientated' environment. As a result I had to make a significant effort to be seen as credible by more technically orientated staff. I found it helpful to spend time with each member of the technical team in order both to learn more of their work and also, vitally, to communicate that I was interested in what they were doing, the challenges they were facing and overcoming, and my respect for and need of them. It is perfectly possible to defer to the expertise of others without losing one's own credibility provided the 'domains' of expertise and, above all, authority are respected.

When it came to selecting a team of Operations Managers via recruitment, a quite different series of challenges presented themselves. What did 'good look like' in a team that did not yet exist?

In this part of my role I made a conscious effort not to rely exclusively on hiring staff who were already experienced call-centre managers. What I sought above all were several key qualities that I knew undoubtedly would more than make up for lack of experience in this particular field.

In each interview I would seek to encourage the individual to identify examples of their ability to 'engage' and identify with a role, and to be 'proactive'.

I needed 'engaged' team members who felt they had a vested interest in the success of the centre, whether it be for personal fulfilment, a career transition or even for promotion. At one point I found myself promoting a woman who had never worked before joining the centre as an agent on the phones. She had been a housewife and mother. She was very quietly spoken, and I remember asking in her interview whether she was at all intimidated at the prospect of managing such a diverse group of people across a broad spectrum of ages and nationalities. I remember well, the 'steel' I glimpsed in her eyes, and the wry smile on her face as she explained that raising three children often called for a firm hand ... She went on to be one of if not *the* best Operations Manager at dealing with 'people issues'.

Good as gold

Another pivotal initiative in creating the call-centre team as a whole – defining its identity and helping to release the latent synergy within it – came in the shape of small plastic badges in the shape of a golden 'Q'. These were known as 'quality' badges. I made it known that any agent achieving a score of 100% for call quality, as measured externally by the client, would be presented with such a badge.

This was an outward and high-visibility method to communicate to everyone what 'good looks like'; showing them the gold.

Some weeks later I enjoyed one of the highlights of my career in call-centre management. I was approached by the duty Operations Manager and together we approached the relevant Team Leader. The agent concerned was on a call and quite oblivious of our presence behind her. But very few of those working there that day were oblivious. Three levels of management stood patiently and quietly behind the young woman's chair, and the more observant may have noticed a bottle of champagne, complete with red ribbon, held in the Operation Manager's hand.

Her call complete, the young woman was approached by her Team Leader, still quite oblivious to our presence, and asked to put her phone on 'divert' so no further calls could come in. The Team Leader then beckoned her to stand and turn round. As she did so, she became aware of us all standing behind her. I could see on her face more than a little trepidation and apprehension. Striving to keep a neutral expression on my face I stepped forward and said I needed to talk to her about the 'quality of her calls'. Holding out a sheet of paper from the client I asked her to read out what it said. I will never forget, as she raised her eyes to mine with, I am quite sure, tears in her eyes, her saying with a huge smile 'One Hundred Per Cent'!

I congratulated her and presented her with the bottle and we all returned to our seats. As I too returned to my desk I knew without any question or doubt that a certain corner had been turned. Few failed to notice that in the coming weeks and months, whatever she wore the young woman always carried that gold 'Q' for all to see.

It was not long before more joined her: visible evidence and examples of what 'good looks like'. Without exception I found these individuals bore within them a certain pride many others would recognise, inspiring them, in turn, to strive so much the harder to deserve their own badge.

This was obviously not merely about the badge, which of itself cost so little, but about what it represented for the wearer and others alike to see. It meant something. It was achievable. It gave those wearing it a certain identity and sense of personal value such as many of them had never had the opportunity to experience before.

In organisations as with individuals there are many diverse 'diseases' that waste and undermine the ability to function. But equally there are many measures to improve health and the unseen 'good bacteria' do much to fight infection and promote health. In organisational life it is a function of the leader to harness such mechanisms; this was surely one.

Establishing two-way communication

Another opportunity arose of both a need and an obstacle – as do many! All agents had access to the client's intranet, which provided both customer data as well as communicating organisation-wide information to all 13 call centres. Unfortunately we had no mechanism via which I could personally communicate with every agent as they did not have e-mail access.

Through negotiation with the client we won the right to set up a local intranet on our server that would in principle allow access to local information and communication to all staff. My next challenge was to find the expertise to implement this. At that time we had a significant number of university students who were working part-time to subsidise their studies. After making some enquiries we soon found we had a team of eager students who would be happy to help design, build and maintain an intranet during periods of low call volumes. This, in turn, was also good for their studies and supported some of their project work. Our intranet soon opened and for the first time we could communicate directly with every agent whether on business or social events we were organising.

However, this was very much a one-way line of communication. In taking over the call centre I quickly realised I had inherited a legacy of bad feeling as a direct result of staff being effectively coerced into shift patterns they did not welcome and which, in many cases, proved impracticable with child-minders, spouses, etc., to take into account.

I remember more than a little consternation among my Operations Managers when I announced that I sought a representative from each team to attend a series of 'forums' to be held coincident with each shift. What caused their apprehension was my stated intent to attend these alone.

I too felt somewhat apprehensive, of course. I was not at all sure as to the reception I would receive from the disgruntled staff. Nevertheless, I was confident it had to be done and entered that hushed, and somewhat negatively charged room, as confidently as I could. From the outset I made it quite clear that these forums were *not* the venue for personal complaints. What I *did* want, however, was to give them a chance to represent and identify any issues they felt had previously gone un-noted or disregarded. On a flip-chart, one by one, we listed and clarified, without discussing or questioning, each issue. With 10 minutes of the allotted hour to go, I asked them to choose the 10 most important items, which I then undertook to address before the next meeting.

Again I knew another turning point had been reached, before even we had done anything about those issues – the important thing was that I had unequivocally shown that I was listening! Over the coming weeks the list grew and then diminished as we addressed each item and communicated to all the outcomes. In some cases (air-conditioning was one), there was not a great deal we could do other than invite agents to change places. In others, such as what the canteen was selling, we met and exceeded expectations.

The most burning issue, however, was that of shift rotas. We addressed this by setting up a separate forum and carrying out a review of all agents to identify preferred shifts. We then communicated exactly what the requirements of our contract were, but that in meeting these we could still offer numerous patterns to accommodate those with demonstrable constraints. Of course in some cases it was still necessary for staff to work relatively unsocial hours periodically, but everyone could see that what could be done to accommodate real difficulties was being done. Above all we demonstrated quite unequivocally that we were 'listening'. At the same time this process gave us a perfect platform to explain exactly what we were doing, and why it was necessary. This was far more successful that the prior situation: people being told what to do with no reason being offered at all.

Facilitating growth

Another problem facing many organisations is that of employees feeling there is no scope for personal growth or development, and nowhere is this truer than in many call centres.

In writing this book I am very conscious of readers, like my own early team leaders, who were promoted for doing a good job as an agent. There was, of course, no guarantee that they would necessarily be a good team leader; they certainly knew how to be a good agent but that was only the start. Once promoted to team-leader status, the individual in question was suddenly expected to demonstrate competence in a wide variety of skills that an agent rarely if ever is called upon to use. Leading, assessing and coaching: all were new, as well as the additional administrative duties with which they would be required to comply.

For this reason I created the role of 'Team Leader Designate'. This role was created so that agents who had demonstrated a willingness and ability to take on greater responsibility were, step by step, encouraged in learning the subsidiary duties of the Team Leader. It also meant we were creating a ready line of succession management and generating back-up in depth for holiday cover etc.

Perhaps the single largest step in developing one's leadership competencies is that very first one – when, for the first time, we take on the mantle of leader. How few organisations cater for the change in outlook necessary for this step!

The bearing of a leader

For many who carry the responsibility of leadership for the first time and unfortunately for many who have led for some time, there is some confusion about the 'bearing' appropriate to good leadership. I remember watching, all unobserved, a new Operations Manager walking across the call-centre floor in full view of everyone on shift – over a hundred people in this case. His head held high, his carriage was more akin to a strut than a walk. His gaze never lowered further than several feet above the heads of the seated agents on the phones. I noticed too the looks of the agents and Team Leaders observing his performance. They were anything but admiring or respectful. The next time I was 'coincidentally' alone with that manager I asked him how often he spoke to agents not on call, and if he knew many of them by name. Such occasions were rare it seemed ... I went on to ask in turn how he thought he was perceived by them. Now he began to falter. I could almost hear the unspoken thoughts of, I suspect, many managers; 'I don't see that it matters what they think of me as long as they do their jobs, and I don't see why I need to know their names'.

With power comes responsibility, and it extends beyond that alluded to in the earlier quote by Dag Hammarskjöld. The manager I described was clearly failing to make an important connection. His being given the badge of office through his 'title' might carry real weight in traditional bureaucracies but increasingly in contemporary organisations management and leadership are by 'consent'. In order to gain more than grudging compliance the leader must be one who gains respect and trust.

Simply by walking across the call-centre floor and meeting the eyes of agents – nodding or sharing a word with those not on a call – communicates an entirely different atmosphere. This extends beyond how a leader walks across a call-centre floor. A good leader will use every opportunity to avoid falling into the trap of only speaking to those from whom he wants something or just to give out fresh 'orders'. It is entirely possible to communicate common humanity and respect without compromising the maintenance of necessary 'distance'. Establishing such trust, relationship and respect building at an early stage goes a long way to making it easier subsequently to ask hard things of those being led. Knowing that the leader genuinely cares makes a huge difference. Staff confidence in leadership cannot help but be undermined if they feel entirely dispensable or anonymous.

Once stranded on the ice of Antarctica, Shackleton was approached to settle the matter of who would get the better goose-down sleeping bags. In order to be entirely fair he had lots drawn and saw to it that neither he nor any officer got one of the better bags! This small subterfuge gained enormous respect from his men and it was even apparent to the officers that the men's increased spirits and hence all their chances of survival were a small price to pay for a less effective sleeping bag ...

Even those uncomfortable times when reprimands are due can offer powerful moments to inspire trust and loyalty. Through hard experience I came to realise something many parents can attest to. When an individual's misdemeanour is reported, the one reporting may, more or less inadvertently, paint a starker picture than reality, or a little more investigation, might bear.

On several occasions I was called to 'deal with' some behaviour that was reported in the bleakest of terms. As the story was related I learned to become aware of emotive language being used to hijack my equanimity as some part of me reacted with greater or lesser degrees of righteous frustration, indignation, anger or even outrage.

If I had been 'wired-up' no doubt one could have observed an increase in respiration and maybe even a slight flush beginning to suffuse my head. But through experience I learned to become ever more alert to early symptoms and primitive responses to emotive language.

At their first emergence it was as if a little voice arose warning me that I was 'losing it'. Soon I responded to such situations by become increasingly 'cool' and detached in my response. As I reached the door to the room where I was to meet the 'miscreant', I made a point of taking a deep breath, putting on a slightly sad smile, and removing any tenseness around my shoulders. Had I been observed by another they might have thought I was squaring up for a fight whereas entirely the contrary was in fact true.

Once seated at eye level – rather than standing over the person in an intimidating way – I would sit beside rather than across a table from them, and express my regret at having had the incident in question brought to my attention. I would then invite the individual to tell me, in their own terms, what had happened and why. Throughout I would avoid being judgemental in word or action.

Such a moment is very telling because the vehemence of denial or sincerity of regret can inform a good leader a great deal as to the appropriate response both to the individual and to the situation. If the person 'comes clean' and acknowledges error then there may well be scope to explore with them how such an incident might be avoided in future whilst an angry response might necessitate further formal investigation. It is no coincidence that in accosting a motorist the police will open conversation with a throwaway comment. This is intended to help them establish what they are dealing with and will inform their response.

By way of illustration I would often tell the story of an Operations Manager who, observing the computer-generated statistics reflecting agent call volumes, durations, etc., noted that one particular agent had taken no calls for over an hour. Filled with 'righteous indignation' the manager stormed across the call centre and disregarding the Team Leader's attempts to understand what was going on, hauled the unfortunate agent into a side office where he proceeded to berate her for failing to take calls. The agent in question weathered the onslaught increasingly sullenly until she could bear it no longer and walked out of the office with the parting comment that she would be delighted to take calls if someone would kindly repair her faulty phone ... It takes little imagination to appreciate the damage that Operations Manager suffered to his reputation, not to mention his embarrassment. It is an object lesson in why it is crucial to gain the facts and listen to both sides of any story before passing judgement.

Playing to team strengths

Every individual in a team has a part to play, but all too often an individual becomes noted for an area of weakness whilst a real strength goes un-noticed. Someone not able to succeed ever as an operator may nonetheless excel as a 'mentor' to novices in whatever sphere. In every case there is real value in sitting down with the non-performer and exploring with them the reasons for this and any ways in which improvements might be gained. This is light-years away from simply setting expectations for punishment and failure.

Regardless, such a reciprocal caring approach is far more likely to elicit ever greater efforts on the part of the individual, whereas the power of fear is more often than not only reflected in ever greater tenseness and the tendency of the individual to 'lock-up' through self-consciousness and fear of failure.

Keeping troublemakers close

Leading a team successfully requires a constant awareness of the ever-shifting chemistry within the team itself as well as the environment in which it operates. In some situations one individual may rise to prominence whilst in another the group will readily defer to another. This tendency of a team to look for a 'spokesperson' other than the leader can be found in the most effective of teams. What Shackleton learned to do was anticipated by Machiavelli many years previously when he said that one should keep his enemies close – to see what they are up to. Shackleton ensured that the troublemakers shared his tent and took the worst of them in his small group that set out from Elephant Island for South Georgia.

Anticipating others' actions and responses to change

Every team is unique and for this reason there is rarely a single approach to gain the best performance, as any football manager can testify. It is therefore vital to observe the team working and to note the all but invisible lines of deference that exist. What engages one individual may in and of itself turn the rest against an idea. The fact that one person suggests an idea may meet with disapproval before its merits are fairly measured. The leaders role here is to seek to anticipate how individuals and the team will react before the event so that a person might be approached privately where appropriate and 'lobbied' for their support. I did this to advantage in a situation where I knew one strong-minded and strong-voiced individual would probably suppress necessary discussion. I spoke with them privately before the meeting and explained that it was important that I gain views from everyone, even those less qualified than him. He remained blissfully low key in the meeting and having found himself presented with a richer picture, was actually amenable to tempering the more extreme view that I knew he would be likely to embrace.

In closing this section on creating a team I would recount a conversation I had with an Operations Manager when I had moved on to another call centre and he had been promoted to act in my place. He was, I think, impressed with what we had achieved together and asked me how I would describe my leadership.

The leader as gardener: the power of empowerment

Sitting there, the metaphor of the gardener sprang to mind. I described entering a beautiful garden where we were met by the gardener who with sweeping grandiloquent gestures showed off the garden he had designed and created. Then

I described a similar situation but where the gardener came forward and showed us around with delight at the beauty of the garden. Praised for his skill a look of astonishment and disbelief crosses his face. He says to us that his part was small. Each and every plant had its own will and place in growing. He points out that he had no part in making the sun shine or the rain fall though he had done what he could to offset the effects of severe frost. All he had really done, he says finally, was to help the garden to grow in a particular way. It would probably have 'grown' all by itself anyway!

As a leader in the complex information-rich organisations of today the traditional leader ruling with an iron hand, retaining all decisions for themselves and exercising complete control, is an anachronism. The speed of change of technology and the volumes of information being processed in a single day today might have taken months or years just 50 years ago. Today's leader needs to be a facilitator. The only way to get maximum performance is by winning the team's collective and individual support, engagement and proactivity. Every decision that can be pushed to the organisation's edges should be. Facilitation should be matched by empowerment circumscribed only by the need to report, by exception, when things are not going well or when trouble is anticipated.

5

Driving change

Anticipating and embracing change

A key function of a leader is to deal with change, and as such they must be as willing to re-orientate themselves to anticipate, identify and deal with new challenges facing the team – as did Shackleton when it became clear he would not only fail to reach the South Pole, but would be fortunate even to survive what lay before him.

Creativity and engagement are the lifeblood of any organisation; they are not a science but a direct product of good leadership. It is not enough to be a successful 'manager' in its limited sense. As the word implies, management suggests 'keeping things going' whereas leadership is all about driving change and innovation, and change and innovation are the very characteristics that define the contemporary world of commerce.

Someone once said that leadership is about doing things right; but leadership is also about doing the right thing. One is about working to the rule book, whereas the other is about throwing it away and breaking new ground, but driven by a vision of the 'right' – what good looks like.

Leadership also depends upon good communication if it is to move from vision to realisation. The success of every organisation, from the family to the global multinational, is dependent upon effective communication. Yet poor communication can also strangle an organisation, bringing it to a grinding halt, if not its knees.

Anyone working in a modern office has probably observed someone, or found themselves, spending hours behind a computer screen digesting e-mails and even sending them to the person at the next desk. The cost of this activity measured in lost productivity is incalculable. This was brought home to me most vividly one day as I sought to wade through over a hundred incoming e-mails.

Opening one, I found a document several pages long, and was perplexed as to why it had been sent to me. I scanned it backwards and forwards, looking for some indication of what was required of me, but to no avail. Feeling a little apprehensive that perhaps I was missing something obvious, and might appear foolish, I walked over to the originator's desk. Opening a general conversation I waited for a suitable moment and mentioned I had noticed an incoming e-mail from them ...

'Oh, that,' they said, '... just thought you should know about such and such'.

'Why's that?', I asked.

'Just in case', they said.

'I see', I replied.

I didn't!

What 'case'?

I could not imagine a 'case' where the information would be of any real value to me at all. After all, there is just so much information 'out there' that 'might' be of value 'some day' that we could never absorb it all ...

I also began to wonder how long the e-mail had taken to write, added to which was the time I could have spent puzzling over it. I realised it was an object example of our ability to be busy rather than productive.

In any position of leadership, communication is vital. But e-mail, in particular, if misguided, can be a terrible drain on time, resources and money. So for everyone, and the leader especially, it is important to recognise when it is far more effective to speak face-to-face.

Information management: management by exception

Equally, good communication is about information management. I soon learned that having established a Management Information System (MIS) one of the greatest challenges was that of identifying just what information we really needed and should, or could, act upon.

Communication is ultimately about the transmission of information, where information is 'significant data: data that matter; that actually make a difference' ... or should!

'Management by exception', and 'exception reporting', quickly became a key focus for the MIS team, as they understood more than anyone that the production of ever greater volumes of unfiltered information was adversely affecting the ability of those receiving it to do their jobs. They were becoming slaves to information and their machines – they were working for information instead of the other way around. We were perilously close to 'paralysis by analysis'. What we needed to do was to ensure the information we received was necessary, information to be acted upon; that the only information we received from the MIS was information we could actually, and needed to, act upon.

Exception reporting

Many organisations fall into a trap: producing so much data about what is 'happening' that it cannot be digested. My response to this problem was to sit down with the MIS team and Operations Managers to identify the relevant exceptions that needed to be reported. Just as some would say 'if it isn't broken don't fix it', so we would say 'if it's working, what you need is information telling you when it is not, rather than simply that it is!'

What we needed to know was when things were going awry and why. We developed a 'dash-board', providing information on performance reflecting our client's service level agreement that was retrospective, real-time and predictive. That was good! Then we refined this further to highlight respective measures only if they showed significant trends requiring attention.

By applying exception reporting, almost overnight, the number of incoming e-mails containing reports and spreadsheets decreased by orders of magnitude. What was communicated was 'information to act upon'. The role of the MIS changed from being one of merely turning out figures by rote to one of analysis and interpretation. This was real job enrichment for the individuals too, and soon we had experts who saw trouble coming far faster than managers, who could easily miss something significant because of the distraction caused by demands on their time by events in the workplace.

Succession management

For many leaders a necessary aid to development and growth comes from the opportunity eventually to move on to new and greater challenges. After all, if one is so good at one's job and even (though unlikely) irreplaceable, what motive is there for senior management to move one?

A retired senior manager once confided to me that in each job he took on he sought as quickly as possible to make his own role 'redundant'. I was understandably mystified by this at first, but he soon explained his logic. During the process of delegation and empowerment, one may soon identify those who are 'engaged and pro-active', those deserving of greater responsibility and trust. This in turn leads to the natural emergence of one's likely successor. At this point, following on from earlier discussion, we can also observe the potential formation of a mentor/mentee relationship.

Known as 'succession management' this process ensures that when a new and (we hope) more appealing role becomes vacant, or when circumstances necessitate the rapid appointment of someone new, no obstacle of our being 'irreplaceable' stands in our way.

Of course, there is some element of personal risk in this approach, but then far fewer people are irreplaceable than they would like to think and if we have successfully reached this point then the job in question will hold little by way of challenge and corresponding reward. In my own case, I successfully achieved this position in my first call centre such that when I was asked as a matter of urgency whether I could move to and take over another call centre – the one already described as needing a 'turn-round' initiative – I was able to do so within a week.

6

The constraints of leadership

The constraint of team and company expectations

An agent repeatedly fails to perform well on calls. Team Leaders and Operations Managers express their 'informed' opinion: this individual 'has to go'. However, upon meeting the individual concerned I was not so sure. Although rather 'abrupt' for customer service and calling a 'spade a shovel' on the phone, they were nonetheless clearly intelligent, educated and certainly willing. I was reluctant to lose someone who was clearly doing their best ... and I was impressed by their forthrightness.

However, I was keenly aware I could 'bend' only so far without being seen as undermining and distrusting my managers on the one hand, and of appearing indecisive and weak on the other, thereby undermining my authority and credibility. I was surprised to find that my freedom to act as I saw fit still had to take into account the perceptions of my team. My answer was to move the individual 'sideways' into a non-customer-facing role where their 'technical skills' came into their own.

I learned that this 'sideways move' can also be a powerful method to move someone out of a role where they are not performing well, without subjecting them to the humiliating and time-consuming process of 'proving incompetence'.

If a good candidate can be identified at the same level as the 'outgoing party', the latter can be approached, suggesting that, as part of the 'job-enrichment' process, you are giving all members of the team an opportunity to develop competence in a variety of roles. This opens the way for a 'shuffling' of roles that, in a crisis, can get the job done in the short term. It also provides a breathing space to deal with the under-performing individual and, of course, opens up the possibility of your finding a role in which they can flourish. A genuine win–win scenario!

Another constraint of leadership was also brought home to me by a situation in which company policies regarding an agent's unacceptable behaviour required me to take stronger measures than I, knowing the person concerned, was inclined to employ. Nevertheless, I realised that making an exception based upon my knowledge of the individual would set a precedent that would return to haunt me as it would undermine my ability to act otherwise and maintain my credibility in future. Understanding a particular individual, or giving them the benefit of the doubt, in a specific circumstance, does not release one from the responsibility of being seen to be consistent when judgements are called for and made.

Through such experiences I learned that as a leader, one must be influenced, to a greater or lesser extent, by the expectations of those one leads.

Any given utterance, decision or behaviour may bear upon the leader's perceived credibility and therefore their ability to merit ongoing trust, respect and loyalty. The demands placed on the leader are like those familiar to celebrities remorselessly pursued by the paparazzi. Every word or gesture, guarded and unguarded, is closely observed and judged.

Sometimes this appraisal and assessment of the leader is conscious and intense, as when we meet a new 'leader' for the first time. There are also those occasions and contexts characterised by uncertainty, when the leader is scrutinised for how they 'bear (and measure) up' to expectations weighing on them as a leader. Most of the time some part of those led stands ever watchful, a silent sentinel, sensitive and alert and ready to 'jump on' anything signalling indecision or weakness.

Many staff criticise leaders for rarely, if ever, owning up to mistakes. I confess that I feel some sympathy for leaders faced with this choice, however. If you truly believe in what you are doing – what you are trying to achieve is for the greater good – then do you give an unscrupulous opponent an opportunity to capitalise upon one mistake that challenges all you seek to accomplish?

Behind the leader's awareness of these expectations is a keen understanding: it takes only one ill-advised action or phrase to undo a thousand good ones! This fact lies behind every leader's general reluctance to admit to error and its implied suggestion of weakness.

People instinctively trust and respect the self-assured leader over those who prevaricate, or appear indecisive and therefore (to them) weak. Of course, many contexts do justify a degree of caution, but the leader must not let this be seen as prevarication. The vast majority of leaders recognise and accept that credibility often turns on their ability to communicate self-assurance and to re-assure the team, no matter what they may feel in the 'wet, dark and cold before the dawn'. Your own uncertainties must remain hidden. Fortunately, I found that in commercial life circumstances are rarely such that an immediate decision is called for. I often disguised my uncertainty under the pretence of seeking further information.

For those inclined to 'wear their heart on their sleeve', this apparent deceit of saying or acting one way, when we feel inclined otherwise, may give pause for thought. Does this mean leaders are liars? Does it mean that leaders are only 'acting'?

Just as we may politely and positively respond to another's well-intentioned 'good morning!' though we may feel it's anything but, so too we must be prepared to exude confidence, self-assurance and decisiveness, no matter what we may 'feel', and despite the 'darkness of uncertainty' through which we might be floundering in the privacy of our own heads and hearts.

It is vital to competent leadership that the varying expectations of individuals and teams are taken into account. To ignore the way they *wish* or *need* to be led often simply leads to misunderstanding and distrust.

Given the importance of our taking account of the expectations of others in order to maintain credibility, and to instil trust and loyalty, the question then is how is this to be done? How can we determine the style of leadership, its attendant behaviours and manner of relating to the team, most likely to succeed?

In our consideration of reflexivity we identified the importance of the leader identifying the strengths, weaknesses, hopes, etc., of those they lead. This cannot happen unless the leader is able to take time to listen and explore these areas with the individual and through careful observation and analysis.

What motivates a particular individual or team in a given context? How well are they performing now, and under what other observed conditions have they succeeded or failed as an individual or as a team? Reflexivity and the ability mentally to transcend the immediate necessities of getting the job done empower the leader to learn from every single encounter with the team and the individuals within it.

The constraint of context

There is no magic formula, no one fixed technique that will assure success in leadership in all contexts. Achieving this competence turns upon our ability to recognise patterns in one context that may be appropriately applied in another.

The organisational manager 'does things right' by the establishment of tried and tested organisational structures and processes. The leader's task differs significantly in that he or she must take account of the unique qualities of a given team, the individuals in it and the context in which it operates to 'do the right thing'. This makes the task of leadership appear far more 'involved' and in many ways less 'mechanical' than that of the manager; that is because it really is! This is not to denigrate or lessen the importance of pure organisational management. It too can be very technically demanding in its own way. Indeed, in reality, today's leader is probably required to embrace the role of both manager and leader, but what this distinction between roles serves to emphasise and clarify is simply the crucial distinctions between them.

One reason why many managerial initiatives, as derived from management courses or books, fail to produce either expected or desired results is arguably their failure to take account of the need for, or deployment of, competent context-appropriate leadership. The effect of this is clearly illustrated by considering the absence, in such initiatives, of due consideration of the specific needs of the team, its individuals and their context.

Taking account of contextual constraints: situational and consensual leadership

Some HR departments still prompt interviewers to ask the question 'How would you describe your leadership style?' Perhaps the best response to such a question in contemporary times is simply 'appropriate'. The notion of the competent leader having 'a *single* leadership style' is a contradiction in terms. The notion of a preferred one-size-fits-all leadership style perhaps reflects a time when leadership was based on rank and having the overt power of sanctions over those led.

For a good overview of contemporary views of 'situational leadership' a good place to start might be *http://www.chimaeraconsulting.com/sitleader.htm* where a model is provided to facilitate understanding as to how leadership style can be tailored to reflect context, and those being led. This model was put together by Ken Blanchard (author of *The One Minute Manager*) and colleague Paul Hersey.

High on the list of priorities for the aspiring leader of today and tomorrow must be a keen awareness that it is not something 'taken' but something 'given', i.e. consented to.

Leadership should not be confused with dictatorship. Compliance gained though fear or the threat of a 'big stick' is not leadership but domination and perhaps dictatorship.

The very nature of leadership has itself continued to change and mature, to reflect a more consensual workplace, the changing nature of society, as well as new sources of power provided by information and other technologies.

With the explosion in websites offering routes to interview and employment there is already evidence that we are just a step away from the employee rather than the employer being the 'consumer'. The success of many companies now includes measures of staff turnover or 'churn'. The significance of such measures is apparent when it is realised that the value individuals represent to companies is now, and increasingly, more about 'personal and intellectual capital' than ever before. In such a climate, individuals are far less likely to tolerate poor leadership, never mind 'dictatorships', and leadership has therefore necessarily become more about facilitating and releasing group potential, rather than 'telling people what to do'.

Transcending the constraints of IQ

Although a high level of intelligence is no prerequisite of good leadership, it cannot of course be entirely 'unintelligent'.

The word 'intelligence' here reflects a core competence of the good leader: an ability to 'read between the lines'. This is no small feat. In any given context the leader must be able to observe accurately, obtain relevant information, draw conclusions, make decisions and persuade others to carry them out. Much of this requires an ability to 'read' others; to infer from what is un-said, as much as from what is; to go beyond the evidence, and to imagine ...

Some might argue that intelligence is itself a fixed mark, as measurable by IQ tests, and that it too is strictly genetic. But increasingly, leadership qualities are reflected in the notion of 'emotional intelligence', as formulated by Irving Goleman, rather than traditional measures of IQ. Based on research carried out by the 'Hay Group', Goleman's notion of emotional intelligence identifies four competencies that characterise the emotionally intelligent person:

- *Self-awareness.* The capacity for understanding one's emotions, one's strengths and one's weaknesses.

- *Self-management.* The capacity for effectively managing one's motives and regulating one's behaviour.

- *Social awareness.* The capacity for understanding what others are saying and feeling and why they feel and act as they do.

- *Relationship management.* The capacity for acting in such a way that one is able to obtain the desired results from others and reach personal goals. (*http://ei.haygroup. com*)

Growing from these basic personal competencies Goleman goes on to identify the following 'basics of emotional intelligence':

- Knowing your feelings and using them to make life decisions you can live with.

- Being able to manage your emotional life without being hijacked by it – not being paralysed by depression or worry, or swept away by anger.

- Persisting in the face of setbacks and channelling your impulses in order to pursue your goals.

- Empathy – reading other people's emotions without their having to tell you what they are feeling.

- Handling feelings in relationships with skill and harmony – being able to articulate the unspoken pulse of a group, for example. (*http://ei.haygroup.com*)

As we have already noted, great leaders are not necessarily the 'sharpest cards in the pack'. They do not need to be, because leaders can only be great *through* others. Good leaders often function in teams more academically qualified, or generally more 'intelligent' or talented in their own fields than they might ever claim or aspire to be. Leadership is not primarily a function of intelligence.

In leadership terms, what may work in motivating a team climbing a mountain or fighting in a war may be entirely inappropriate in the workplace. The unreasoned transposition of leadership styles from one context to another is therefore probably doomed to failure. Certainly, one can, as much of this book suggests, learn from the experiences of leaders whether mythical, metaphorical, real, historical or contemporary, but the patterns of leadership in each context must be filtered to discern their relevance for other individuals, teams and contexts.

This ability to learn from experience is something every functioning mature adult has developed; it is not necessarily confined to the sphere of leadership. What the leader does though is to develop a focus on what characterises successful leadership in one unique context and to 'graft' what is relevant to another, discerning what is unique both in the source situation and where it is to be applied.

It is not difficult, for example, to realise that Shackleton's style of leadership was exceptionally successful on the Antarctic ice. We can then ask, 'what is there about that unique context, and those individuals in history, that can be extracted and applied more generally by the leader?'

Shackleton did something to achieve his result. Through all he said and did, he communicated a genuine optimism as to their chances of survival, and together with his care for the team he achieved a reciprocal level of optimism in the crew and their abiding loyalty to him. The specifics of how he did this may well not be either relevant or applicable in a contemporary context, such as his manner of distributing sleeping bags described earlier.

Nevertheless, we *can* learn that appropriate actions and words transmit optimism and care for the team. Whatever relevant words or deeds are identified in another context, it is certain that failure to address this need would have found Shackleton, and any leader, and whether the 'ice' is metaphorical or real, foundering and very much alone.

In closing this section on the loneliness of the leader and the significance of subordinates' expectations, it is also worthwhile acknowledging that the leader's own leader will have expectations that are also a significant factor influencing if not governing priorities and behaviour.

The constraint of fallibility: from the worst to the best – learning from mistakes

This account of my personal initiation into and experiences of leadership would be less than honest if it suggested that I made no mistakes. A hard-earned lesson of experience for me arose paradoxically out of my dedication to the immediate challenges of leadership within my call centre.

The manager and leader may have many stakeholders: those with an active 'interest' in what the organisation does, and how it is done. For me they included staff, customers, the client and my own employer. In terms of balancing and striving to meet these often competing interests, my success often took the form of what management literature refers to as 'satisficing'; that is, doing just enough to satisfy immediate expectations or demands.

The stakeholder's expectations I focused upon too exclusively were those of the client, the customers on the end of the phones and my internal staff. It seemed a worthy and appropriate focus: the task in hand was to 'turn round' an unsatisfactorily performing call centre and make it productive and profitable. Unfortunately this total focus on the job at hand resulted in my failure to 'manage up', to ensure that both the call centre and my own profile were consistently kept 'on the radar' of those outside my immediate environment.

I was aware that regular 'external' meetings were held between other managers. These often semisocial 'networking' events were held often some distance away from my call centre. For my part, I felt at the time that my participation in these was a distraction from and would not much contribute to my own performance in what was a demanding environment, where days away from the call centre carried a cost I did not feel was justified. I was wrong.

Unfortunately for me, in the 'real' world, my absence was not interpreted in the light of my genuine motives but by others with their own axe to grind. Some undoubtedly felt there was personal mileage in 'supposing' out loud that my absence reflected my less than committed attitude to the 'larger team' of which we were all a part.

The end result was that when the totally unexpected occurred, and my part of the organisation was outsourced to another company, my negative profile outside the call centre meant a less than favourable impression was transmitted to the incoming management by those with a vested interest in the elevation of their own profile.

Although I had rightly focused on the 'downward' demands of my leadership position it should not have been at the expense of failing to 'manage up, and out'. The importance of networking is not simply a matter of self-interest and self-promotion though. I realise in retrospect that there would be real benefits to such networking and perception management because, in the absence of my input, others raised their own profile to the detriment of not just me but also the part of the organisation I represented. This in turn led to a situation where, in competition for resources, my area probably 'missed out' because others made the effort to make their case. So both I and my team suffered as a result of this failure on my part.

The constraints of delegated leadership – the need to set limits

I was keenly aware that with my call centre operating from 7 a.m. to 10 p.m. every day of the week, I simply could not be in personal attendance all of the time.

Like a ship's captain I needed to be able to rely on the 'officer of the watch' to make sound decisions in my absence. I did not want someone who would come running to me to ask permission to change course around an iceberg, but I certainly expected them to come running if a flapping 'skull and crossbones' loomed over the horizon! This is another reason why delegation is crucial to success. But along with that delegation of responsibility must go a clear awareness of what the delegate has and has not the power to do. It is thus vital that if staff are to be empowered, time is set aside to anticipate every practicable contingency that they may be faced with and the point at which they are obliged to 'escalate' the problem to their superiors in the organisation.

Another incidental benefit which delegation offers that greatly facilitates the leader's own development and progression is its part in succession management, the personal benefits of which we discussed previously.

With so many demands on the leader's time being all too apparent, how could I ensure my time and efforts were not squandered? What makes for a productive rather than a merely 'busy' leader? As personal productivity is enhanced through delegation and empowerment, how did I ensure that the personal productivity and effectiveness of subordinates were also maximised through good time management?

7

The unforgiving minute: from busyness to working smart

The title for this chapter takes us back to Rudyard Kipling, who gave us the 'six honest serving men' alluded to earlier, but this time to the final words of his famous poem 'If':

> If you can fill the unforgiving minute
> With sixty seconds' worth of distance run,
> Yours is the Earth and everything that's in it,
> And – which is more – you'll be a Man, my son!

Kipling's verse, written long before women achieved anything like their current state of emancipation, reflects his perception of 'manhood' but what the imaginary father is entreating his son to take account of is as vitally important to today's leader, man or woman, as it ever was.

We have already touched upon the ways in which ill-conceived meetings can un-necessarily eat up time and money and the 'opportunity costs'; the opportunities 'lost' through attendees not being elsewhere and doing other things. Most of us can remember countless times and hours seated mute, unable to do anything productive, and yet feeling surplus to the needs of a discussion or meeting.

This is not to denigrate the very real value of bringing people together in the same room, whether physically or virtually, for a well-focused productive meeting. It *is* important that we are able to shake hands with colleagues we may work with, but see rarely, and it *is* important to spend time in some superficially spurious if not banal chit-chat, because this is a fundamental way of getting to know each other and, as we have seen, getting to know others is a precursor, especially for the leader, to good and effective communication.

From 'busy' to productive

As a senior management assessor for the National Vocational Qualification (NVQ) Programme, I often visited organisations where, like the 'invisible' person behind a pub bar, I would hear staff come together and converse at length, perhaps for half an hour or more. Sadly, the outcome of such conversations in terms of action being taken was often questionable. Yet, when approached on matters genuinely requiring attention and action, how often would the reply be 'Oh, sorry, I am just too busy'. Sadly, and ironically, in many cases I think the individuals concerned genuinely thought this was true.

It can be salutary from time to time to pull ourselves up short and ask 'what have I achieved or changed today? What difference has my being here made?' In an early Operations Managers' meeting I caused a considerable degree of discomfort by posing the question 'What am I paying you for?'

The discomfort my question gave rise to came from the fact that all too often we lose sight of this as a priority. It is in the light of this question that we should develop a self-disciplined focus on asking, every day: 'what do I want, and need, to achieve today?' If we honestly did this daily – allowing the question to prompt our identifying 'SMART' objectives for each day, for both our work and our personal time, then I have no doubt that our lives would be far richer, vital and, of course, more productive on every level.

Again, if you find yourself leading a group or a meeting and want to get someone's attention, try asking them to consider what they have 'achieved today' – or put another way, what value they have brought into the company to justify their pay?

When I saw a problem being addressed by calling a meeting I often took a little time to consider its cost benefits. At one time such meetings would necessitate hotel and even airfare costs as well as the cost of my time and others in meetings. When all this is added up it can soon become apparent that the benefits sought by a meeting need to be quite substantial to justify the costs incurred. These are the direct costs of the meeting but in addition it may well be that opportunities for doing more productive work are also lost.

Personal effectiveness and productivity for today's leader have been significantly enhanced by the need to drive responsibility down the hierarchy, empowering staff in ways previously unheard of. Not long ago, one individual could effectively 'think' for, and give orders to, large numbers of individuals. In such times competition was not as fierce, and the sociological, technological, economic and political environments were relatively stable.

By contrast, today's leaders often find themselves working in an environment changing so rapidly and on so many of these 'fronts' that no single person could possibly make all the decisions that successful competitive commerce ruthlessly demands.

Mention has already been made of the value of exception reporting, because of its role in reducing the amount of

that needs to be, should be and can actually
on. A similar process needs to be taken by the
determining the level of their involvement in
aking.

ason that leaders such as Hitler, thankfully, failed
spirations was their inability to 'let the experts do
then . '. Hitler's insistence in attempting to invade Russia
in winter, for example, despite the protestations of his
generals who understood what was involved, exemplifies
this. As leader today, it is important to determine the levers
over which to retain control and those which can be
'delegated', i.e. those that others can be 'empowered' to
operate. The two key words here are 'delegation' and
'empowerment'. Established appropriately, an organisation
becomes tremendously responsive and adroit in meeting the
challenges of a volatile competitive commercial environment. This applies whether it be the ability of a salesperson
to negotiate a deal within set parameters, rather than trying
to operate on a fixed price, or the agent in a call centre
empowered to provide incentives to a potential or existing
customer. In both cases the scope for applying informed and
intelligent initiative can result in the difference between
winning or losing business of a value many orders of
magnitude beyond any immediate costs incurred.

As leader and manager it is vital that one's personal
workload is managed to ensure that as much of the routine
decision-making is 'pushed' down the line of command as
practicable. Relevant provisos and exceptions can be
defined, such that the leader is not surprised by someone
stepping 'over the line' and assuming more responsibility
than a context or their remit justifies.

Carried out effectively, such delegation and empowerment
also carries the benefits of creating more fulfilling and
enriched roles for subordinates, which also encourages their

greater 'engagement' in their work. It also frees up the leader to focus on the many areas of leadership activity I have highlighted.

The greatest steps forward in my understanding of meeting leadership came early in the days I worked with Kate, my mentor. It is to this aspect of time management, as a cure for mere 'busyness', that I now turn, before going on to look at broader techniques of time management as a vital competence in the leadership toolkit.

The unforgiving minute in public: Kate and meetings

In each business context I observed my mentor Kate operate in – usually chairing multidisciplinary meetings of programmers, consultants, systems analysts, salespeople, account managers, etc., Kate was, as ever, incredibly focused. Initially most people, including myself, were unsettled by her direct, some would say 'blunt', approach to the management of meetings.

But no one questioned her effectiveness. The digressions and political smokescreens I saw exhibited elsewhere were notably absent when Kate was in charge. She had an uncanny knack of cutting through spurious, peripheral or irrelevant arguments, getting to the nub of any issue and addressing it head-on. In particular, at the heart of this process she deployed a technique that invariably brought clarity to the most apparently complex situations.

Anyone with experience of business meetings has 'been there'. One after another, interested parties contribute and debate 'around' an issue. Some, we recognise, contribute more to make their own presence and self-importance felt, rather than any concern with achieving a solution. Others are either too mired down in the detail or else too abstract and high-level in their thinking to offer concrete actions or solutions. It is the classic case of the conversation oscillating between a focus on the 'trees' and the 'wood', each perspective throwing up often conflicting priorities to which reconciliation seems impossible.

Sitting in a meeting led by Kate, I would often become confused, as the initial issue was grasped and manipulated by individuals with conflicting takes and interests, and moulded to reflect their own more-or-less explicit ends or priorities. It was like being in a courtroom or political debate where, almost despite oneself, one agrees by turns with quite conflicting portrayals of issues, individuals and events. I suspect most of us have 'been there' too.

Yet when, sooner or later, Kate intervened, her approach and words held the precision of the surgeon's scalpel: shearing away extraneous argument, leading inexorably to clear understanding and agreement on what was to be done, by whom, why, how and when.

How did she do it? This first mystified and then intrigued me for some time, until eventually I became aware of a distinct pattern to her leadership and control over meetings.

Kate was ensured of her leadership success in meetings before she entered the room, and when she did, by ensuring the management of the meeting was duly attended to.

First, I could be sure that if I was invited to participate in a meeting it meant just that; there was always a good reason for my being there. An agenda, with previous minutes where relevant, always arrived in good time for the meeting itself, which was arranged with sufficient notice to ensure all could attend, duly prepared for their part in it.

The agendas produced by Kate always carried a specific time allotted to each subject, and in most cases the issues that could be addressed relatively quickly came first. Then the core issues followed, with the greatest proportion of the available time allotted to them.

During informal meetings Kate would sometimes do the timekeeping and minute-taking herself, but where larger issues were under discussion or in higher level management meetings she would often delegate these tasks. Regardless, she would ensure that each subject kept to its allotted timeslot as far as practicable. Of course, some subjects could turn out to be more involved than had originally been expected but in such cases Kate found ways to 'park' issues for consideration in a separate meeting, or identify a group of relevant people to meet separately and report back to the main group with their findings or for decision-making purposes.

To fail in any one of these 'mechanics' of meeting preparation or management would inevitably lead to poor time management or meeting over-runs.

Once the meeting began, Kate began by clearly going over the reasons for it having been called, ensuring that everyone understood and agreed with its purpose and objectives. From there on, she addressed the very same 'key questions' outlined earlier which, I came to realise, characterised her approach, whether leading and managing meetings or elsewhere.

The ubiquitous all-encompassing power of those four questions consistently guide me in almost every unique managerial and leadership context I find myself in, or am challenged by. When academic models seem to offer no way forward, I invariably find a way ahead through application of these four questions. Whenever I am not sure what to do next, I still turn to them for insight and guidance and assurance that all is well.

1. *What are we trying to achieve?* This applies to the meeting as a whole, as well as to issues within it.

2. *What does 'good' look like?* What factors must a decision or solution take account of?

3. *Where are we now?* What are the relevant characteristics of the current situation that reflect where we are in relation to our objective?

4. *How do we get from 'here' to 'there'?* What must we do, who should do it and what obstacles need to be overcome? What is the appropriate means to our end?

Kate encouraged each person to contribute. On occasion she would draw out a line of reasoning, or invite participation from those more reticent. Her approach was invariably inclusive yet, under the scrutiny of her focus and analysis, I learned to be concise and to think things through. It was always dangerous to trot out some unexamined or 'accepted' wisdom.

However, there were occasions when it was appropriate to 'dilate' the discussion and to 'think outside the box'. When a problem was outlined and objectives clarified and agreed, Kate would use the brainstorming technique in order to introduce some degree of lateral thinking that would generate original perspectives and solutions.

A powerful brainstorming technique Kate employed was to seek or suggest a scenario bearing oblique similarities to the problem at hand. For example, in exploring alternative methods of organisation, she might invite or suggest the variety of ways in which various living creatures organise themselves. This could lead, for example, to consideration of the ways ants or termites organise themselves, how wolves hunt in packs, or how herding cats might be achieved! In this last case, for example, it is quickly apparent the approach must take account of cats' instinctive lack of inclination to group together, their fear of dogs and their appetite for fish! One possible strategy might therefore be to focus not on the herding as such, but rather on the mechanisms that might be employed to create an incentive each individual cat will be drawn to, or to create a sense of threat they will shy away from and hence towards each other. The permutations are endless. Once a diverse variety of scenarios have been created in the minutes set aside, the next task was to translate these insights in a way that cast light on the original problem. In this example, having discovered that a particular group of people are 'as hard to herd as cats', enhanced appreciation that where people have no immediate tendency to bond, they might do so under conditions of a commonly perceived and understood threat, or where individual objectives are aligned with those of the group. In concrete terms this example served to highlight for us the need to ensure that the team appreciated the reason for our encouraging them to take up an initiative – to move in a particular direction. We realised that metaphorically waving our arms around to drive them along was far less effective than being able to communicate in a way they could relate to.

In these brainstorming sessions, Kate was able to encourage the group to let go their discriminating and critical faculties in the time set aside for this phase, and to offer wild but often surprisingly insightful perspectives, whilst she maintained firm control over the process as a whole. Again, she would seek contributions from all, and suppress any one individual from dominating the discussion, or from being critical when unfettered thought was to be encouraged.

It was intriguing to observe. It could also be unsettling. You could find yourself unexpectedly the focus of attention as your own, previously un-volunteered opinion or contribution was sought. Knowing you would probably be asked for an opinion was a very effective way to encourage engagement in the process. Unsurprisingly perhaps, I soon realised my opinion was often sought precisely when Kate perceived, by observing my eyes or body language, that I was starting to 'drift', and was not paying due attention to the proceedings at hand, or to the contributions of others.

Kate's ability in the often hectic 'to and fro' of debate in meetings, to anticipate and respond to (rather than reacting to) various arguments that arose, made her preparation for meetings very apparent. From her, I learned to consider, anticipate and prepare responses to the arguments of those dissenters. As a result, on occasion I approached specific attendees prior to a meeting, and lobbied them for support or appreciation of what I sought to achieve. If I thought one individual might dominate proceedings, I could usually get them to tone down their contribution by explaining that I needed to take account of the views of less vocal participants. This mirrored the Machiavellian approach employed by Shackleton, as mentioned earlier, of keeping potential enemies close at hand.

Each technique described so far assists in good time management in meetings.

Managing and leading meetings is like managing and leading in a scaled-down version of the organisation at large. It is not surprising therefore that the 'four questions' are equally powerfully there. Just as the leader should prepare carefully for a meeting to ensure its smooth running, so time spent preparing in private for the implementation of plans can save a great deal of time that is wasted unnecessarily through a failure to anticipate contingencies beforehand.

The unforgiving minute in general leadership

In my early days as call-centre manager, I vividly remember occasions when I would arrive in the morning and it might take an hour to reach my own desk. This was a good example of poor time management resulting from managing others badly. Someone would often accost me with the request for a 'minute' of my time that would often escalate – for which read 'spiral out of my control' – into something taking considerable longer.

Eventually I realised this just would not do. Accordingly, the next time I was approached in this manner I answered positively and, urgency permitting, would assign a specific time to meet later in the day. This approach progressed as I established a 'surgery hour' at a time convenient to me. Furthermore, I made it clear that, with time at a premium, I would expect my staff to have thought through the nature of their problem such that they could succinctly 'headline' the issue and where they saw my part (and theirs) in addressing it.

This simple initiative led to a dramatic improvement for me, not least because by encouraging others to define their issue clearly, and our respective roles in addressing it, they would often 'happen' upon the answer, and importantly their own part in it, themselves.

Similarly, where my immediate and direct involvement was justified, I would 'avoid like the plague' scenarios where I would metaphorically 'roll up my sleeves' and deal with it all myself, whilst the person bringing the problem sat back and 'smoked a cigar' while I 'floundered around in the swamp, up to my navel in alligators!' In such situations I always sought to involve the person concerned directly, such that where appropriate they would, in future, be able to deal with the issue themselves. Also, where general precedents were set or lessons learnt, I ensured they were communicated to all other relevant colleagues, be they team leaders or operation managers.

This approach contributes to what is often termed 'organisational learning': short-cutting the process whereby everyone makes the same mistakes in order to learn the same lessons – a huge waste of time. Establishing good processes of communication and debriefing after all significant events (good and bad) or projects helps to save significant amounts of time for all.

8

Touching base: it's good to talk

Competent communication lies at the heart of every leader's ability to achieve success.

Nothing can happen until the gap between what is in the head and heart of the leader and those being led is effectively bridged. No matter how brilliant the leader's ideas, no matter how great their grasp of their craft, no matter how learned, educated or how qualified they are, they are without value unless the leader communicates effectively.

Communication takes place via a variety of media: one-to-one or one-to-many verbal, typed, hand-written, electronic; by e-mail, fax, telephone or video. That's quite a range and a lot of discrete competencies to consider for the aspiring leader. But competence in each of these media must be preceded by competence in deciding which medium is going to be most effective and appropriate if the desired outcome of communication is to be realised.

The time potentially wasted in meetings and sending spurious e-mails has been considered. But how does one decide the appropriate medium – what criteria for choice are relevant? In most cases the easiest way to get the right answer in choosing an appropriate medium is to consider the required 'effect or outcome': what do you want to achieve?

E-mails and all written documentation capture what has been said. In today's data-sensitive organisations this can be a blessing or a curse as many politicians and organisations have discovered to their cost and chagrin. For the leader, the written word ensures that any subsequent debate about what has been said can be readily resolved. The communication of significant agreements and objectives should therefore always be written.

In considering what is to be communicated and the appropriate medium, it can be helpful for the leader to put themselves in the position of the recipient. 'How would I feel if someone wrote this to me, or said it to me in private, or in front of others?' In the next chapter I will specifically address the leader's task in meeting and dealing with the inevitable conflicts that arise in any organisational context. But it is quite obvious that poor communication has the ability to cause more problems than good communication can solve.

I remember one manager being subjected to a vitriolic response from a local government official who had received a letter in which the manager had meant to write something to the effect of: 'The problem arose as a direct result of actions taken by your people'. Unfortunately the letter 'r' had somehow not made it onto the written page, leading to: 'The problem arose as a direct result of actions taken by *you* people'. The effect of reading the latter is readily apparent. Notably, even a spell-check run on the letter would not have picked up this glaring and unfortunate error.

The lesson is clear. In composing any sensitive document, it is wise to re-read it or, where possible, get someone trustworthy to 'proof-read' it. It is amazing how the writer's eye misreads to offer only what it 'expects' to find. A classic example of this follows: 'I'll look forward to seeing you, when we finally meet, in Paris, in the the Spring' – where the eye slides so easily over the repetition of 'the'.

In today's automated world of word processing, spelling and grammar checks, there is no excuse for simple spelling errors. Yet how often these life-savers are turned off or disabled for convenience: some convenience, when one considers the potential for damage, misunderstanding and embarrassment.

Like the actor, a leader should always be sensitive to the *actual* effect of their communications, which may well be very different to that intended. Similarly the leader, like a sports coach, may benefit from recognising that what people '*need* to hear' may in fact contrast sharply with 'what they *feel* like saying'.

Constant attention to how people react and respond to communication can be most revealing. It is as well to remember that we were blessed at birth with two ears, two eyes but only one mouth. In the realm of communication it may be good to talk but it is often better to listen.

For the leader, communication is very much about being able to read between the lines of what people 'say' or 'do not say', 'do' or 'do not do'.

Earlier discussion raised the value of understanding what does, or does not, motivate people. By paying close attention to the way others behave, respond and react, valuable insights into their state of mind, attitudes, engagement, degree of proactivity, energy levels, etc., can effectively be inferred.

Competent leaders pick up numerous tell-tale signs or signals, known by behavioural scientists as 'tells', simply by being observant in even the most transient of encounters: observing whether another's body language, tone, pitch and pace of voice, state of dress, general smartness, etc., confirm what they are saying or contradict it.

Specialists in this area now believe that for the majority of the population, distinct 'tells' in behaviour can signal unwitting inconsistencies between what is said by an individual and what they really think or feel. For the leader to become sensitised to deviations in behaviour it helps enormously if they have become acquainted with individuals' general behaviour and use of language over time.

Competent leaders do not shy away from acknowledging the impact and significance of first impressions though. Although recognising the dangers of prejudice, they will take account of their own trained and nurtured ability to 'pick-up' on numerous less-than-obvious indicators such as the way one moves, speaks or behaves that often elude conscious perception. It sounds more complicated than it is. It is simply about acknowledging one's gut-instinct as a valuable, but not exclusive, contributor to our assessment of others. Our noted subliminal perceptions and inclinations simply serve as a precursor to the next step, which is to explore and test these instincts through discussion with the individual concerned as well as, quite possibly, colleagues and, where relevant, subordinates and bosses.

As call-centre manager, I was always conscious that the face turned toward me by subordinates at every level was probably a different one to that turned towards others. An operation manager who might present a reasonable and tolerant face to me might possibly turn a more tyrannical one to their subordinates.

I was also aware that 'perception management' could be used on me by my own subordinates. An individual would seek to win me over to a particular view by presenting or suppressing facts as suited their purpose. It has probably been like this from the time of the very first leaders (and parents). It can also seem very flattering. It is one thing to denigrate others as sycophants, but if the vast majority of those around you come to defer automatically, or out of any fear of being punished for *not* seeming to do so, it is easy to be lulled (or gulled) into a sense of infallibility: to believe everyone unquestioningly accepts your view of things. Ironically, the more one is feared, the more likely it is this phenomenon will arise.

The value of dissent and the danger of repressing it

Competent leaders therefore accept it is neither unusual nor wrong to find decisions challenged or unpopular, and accept the presence of 'managed' dissent or challenge – from time to time. If the 'spice' of dissent is allowed to reveal itself in a controlled manner, the leader has an invaluable guide to the 'pulse' of their organisation, and teams. It is rather like being able to observe and hear steam gently hissing through the release valve on a pressure cooker. If it is silent, then nothing at all may be happening inside, but ...

Perhaps it is better not to silence voices of dissent or challenge entirely. For such voices are invaluable guides to health, just as human physical reflexes indicate the general health of a patient to the doctor.

What constitute 'issues' for staff may not be immediately apparent to the leader, and may not even appear on their own 'radar'. Such was the case in the earlier described forums, established to ascertain, vent and address staff issues. While the leader may be seeking to address and reconcile issues of cost and quality, staff may be on the verge of revolt because there are no salads in the canteen, or the air conditioning is too cool. The only way to find out about such issues is to ask, and then to be seen to be doing something about it.

Competent communication is also about ensuring that, when something good is *not* possible or something bad is happening to, or required of, staff, they are given the benefit of an explanation. Few would launch themselves willingly out of a trench and into a hail of machine-gun bullets without good reason, but many would, if convinced by the value of some 'higher good'.

Just as the engineer is constantly attuned to the tone and rhythm of the engines in their care, so too the leader develops an ability to scan subordinates for significant signs beyond the basic words of conversation, or communication itself. In this area the value of one-to-one and face-to-face communication reveals far more to the leader than could be expected in a more public situation. Leaders confining themselves to public appearances and meetings are likely to end up misjudging the mood and sensibilities of those they lead.

For the leader to lose touch with the 'pulse' of those they lead is as detrimental as for the doctor to lose touch with the pulse, not to mention blood pressure, of their patient.

Another key area of communication, or rather a lack of it, leading to many organisational dysfunctions is the failure to carry out staff performance review and career development sessions with employees. This applies equally to all organisations, large or small, private or public sector.

Staff performance review and career development

Most of our communications within an organisational context are one-to-one or one-to-many; they concern the people involved. The context of staff performance review and career development, however, incorporates another dimension as they represent a communication between the 'organisation' and the individual personally. Although some degree of informality is usually encouraged to facilitate discussion, both parties are aware on some level that in this 'space' there is a dialogue between themselves and the organisation. It is therefore vital that they are carried out with due gravity and propriety. The presence of such communication, on a regular basis, is vitally important.

For management, especially in organisations with large spans of control, such formal reviews can of course represent a significant overhead in terms of time and effort, and this can be reflected in dismissive attitudes towards them and their being relegated in the light of apparently more pressing operational demands.

Such attitudes are hardly conducive to effective staff performance review and career development meetings. But for the employee their absence can signify many things, from a perception that the company has 'lost its way and is spiralling out of control' to perhaps one of the most damaging perceptions an employee can have of their employer: that they 'just don't care'. This lack of care is especially damaging because if the employer is not seen to care, then sooner or later the employee will, in most situations, begin to wonder why *they* should care about the job – even if they go through the motions for a pay-slip.

At the other end of the scale, motivated and successful employees begin to suffer from a gnawing doubt that the reason that these processes have been dropped, if they ever existed, is because the company is seeking to duck the issue of fair reward for their effort, commitment and success.

Given the multiplying damage caused by *not* having a due process of performance assessment and career development, the need for this formal process is glaringly apparent.

The 'bottom line' is that *no* organisation can sustain any argument against their being established and conscientiously adhered to.

The absence of this platform for communication also raises serious questions about the degree to which senior management can be confident that each employee understands 'what good looks like', for them personally within the context of the company's strategy and objectives as a whole. It is one thing for a manager to ascribe tasks on a short-terms basis, but such an approach, in isolation, is reminiscent of the soldier expected to leave the trenches and advance with no clear understanding as to why, and therefore no ready source of motivation for doing so.

This not being a book on management but rather 'practical leadership', the mechanics of performance and career review are not addressed in detail; there is an abundance of courses, written, audio and visual material readily available to meet such needs. What *is* of specific relevance, for the practical leader, is a clear understanding of the penalties for not establishing this vital medium of communication between the organisation and the employee, as well as the excellent platform it provides for establishing organisational objectives and priorities as they relate to each and every unique employee. As a leader, bow to any pressures to delay these reviews or even worse fall prey to the trap of thinking they are an 'un-necessary overhead' at your peril. To do so will surely lead to some or all of the penalties indicated above.

Leadership is about creating motivation through inspiration and perspiration, but it is important to realise that it can be equally damaging and counter-productive to over-inflate expectations, or to set objectives, the fulfilment of which is questionable.

There should be congruence between the objectives and priorities set for teams and individuals, and those of the organisation as a whole, and the prospect of their achievement must be carefully assessed and realistic. 'Setting people up to fail' simply de-motivates and leads to a cynical and jaundiced view as to the credibility of those setting the targets. It is all very well to fail, aiming for the stars, and still reach the moon, but if the latter has not also been established and acknowledged beforehand as a legitimate target or stepping stone to success, the endeavour will be perceived as a failure.

When the organisation or some part of it is failing to achieve, or generally performing poorly, the leader, as with the frustrated parent or coach, may well wish to scold or admonish. The competent leader must develop an ability to transcend this impulse and to consider what approach will best produce the results they desire.

Undoubtedly the 'stick' may sometimes offer more hope of success than the 'carrot' but the former always carries a cost. There may be times when admonishment is expected, but disruption of this expectation by offering understanding, tolerance and encouragement has been known to lead to the team or individual's fundamental re-appraisal of their leader and organisation. The necessary discernment necessary to such a choice of approach is not just a gift that some leaders undoubtedly have. Such discrimination between alternatives is invariably directly related to the leader's developed and informed knowledge of the team and individuals in it. The only way therefore to develop such an ability to do the 'right thing' is to know and understand what works with particular teams and the individuals within them. Such understanding cannot take place from behind an office wall or a computer screen. Long before a crisis emerges the leader should have taken time to get to know those for whom they are responsible.

There were occasions in managing those hundreds of call-centre staff when an issue would arise akin to the situation in which a child carries out an act quite simply to 'provoke a response'. In such situations it is all to easy to 'react' and thereby send out precisely the signal sought by the offender: that you are 'out of control' or 'losing it'. Such times demand a precisely measured response. Examples of such situations that come to mind are where individuals began to test the dress code – a notoriously difficult policy to police, particularly in high summer or deep winter – or where employees failed to observe common courtesy in leaving wash-rooms in an acceptable state of cleanliness.

In such situations it is all too easy to deploy stern warnings and 'polite notices' but such measures can easily degenerate to the point where leadership is perceived to be 'over-reacting', again sending out signals that things are out of control. It is worthwhile simply to remember that 'sending in the troops' to cavalry or 'baton-charge' a crowd of protesters often merely serves to destabilise the situation further. The ability to provoke such a response is held as a victory by those wishing to reveal the iron fist lurking beneath a velvet glove; 'the organisation pretends to care, but step out of line and you get squished!'

Where leadership presents itself as benevolent, its credibility as such can be severely undermined if some minority succeed in any initiative that evokes a draconian response. It is important to respond rather than submitting to instinctive knee-jerk reactions. In the case of flaunted dress codes, it may be practicable during seasonable peaks to offer some compromise taking account of the need for staff to be reasonably comfortable, whilst discouraging the effects of scantily clad staff on professional appearances to outsiders and internal standards of behaviour.

The 'hygiene' factor was also addressed by a graduated response that began with a low-key communication focussing not on 'management displeasure' at standards being compromised etc., but rather highlighting the effects of such behaviour for the staff themselves. This also encouraged the development of an ethos that was actually self-policing, which was all to the good, and actually served further to develop a sense of team identity not based on us (staff) against them (management), but rather on us (staff) against those who do not respect our own working environment.

As was shown at the outset of this chapter, communication constitutes the principal medium by which the competent leader realises their vision of 'what good looks like'. It is a fundamental indicator of organisational health that every employee understands their part in organisational strategy through a clear appreciation of their personal and team objectives and priorities. Communicating and maintaining this understanding is a primary function of the leader and the tools to accomplish it will vary depending on the context.

In conclusion:

- understand and get to know the team and its constituent members,
- have a clear vision of objectives and priorities at every level,
- discern what should or should not be communicated,
- discern the appropriate medium of communication, and
- take 'measured steps' – respond but avoid 'knee-jerk' reactions.

This discussion on communication has largely been concerned with the day-to-day running and leadership of a team. In reality, however, there are times 'when the wind blows' and 'storms lash', threatening much that at other times is stable and secure. In the next chapter we turn to the unique benefits of leadership over pure management in such situations.

9

Storms of passage: leading through conflict

Adversity defines us as human beings and leaders. It strips away any option of relying on established routine, responses or policies. When circumstance demands the leader to forge order from chaos he or she is forced back upon the very competences of practical leadership this book focuses upon.

Conflict arises between people, between organisations or as competition in a commercial environment; this may be physical, sociological, psychological or political. As discussed earlier, external conflict can also precipitate and magnify pre-existing inner personal conflicts. For the leader in particular, adversity and conflict will reveal, as little else does, their true fibre, ability and worthiness to lead others. If they are not masters of themselves, they will likely find self-doubts as to their purpose, their ability, or both, amplified.

The uncentred leader – one flawed by inconsistencies between what they claim to be and are – finds every flaw and inconsistency magnified and they are therefore that much harder to deal with.

In short, the leader's immersion in conflict emphasizes the fact that true leadership is not a 'job'. Those inclined towards over-controlling subordinates find it increasingly difficult to facilitate and empower others as adversity and conflict arises, and more tempted to draw more and more decision-making inwardly to themselves. Conversely, those who are inclined to prevarication and indecisiveness will find themselves increasingly caught, like the proverbial rabbit in the headlights of an oncoming vehicle, powerless to deal with the demands for decisions rushing towards them from all sides.

The necessary groundwork enabling a leader to cope with all the challenges inherent in conflict situations begins with the patient unremitting practice of self-discipline. Emotional intelligence or maturity cannot be learned from a book. It is first and foremost about the aspiring leader developing competence in dealing effectively with conflict internally, before seeking to deal with what is external.

In practice, this is exemplified in the most basic of conflict situations faced by the leader. Something happens externally that 'instinctively' evokes in us feelings of outrage, anger, fear, all three or more; how do we cope? It is all very well for a book to say we should approach the situation calmly and objectively, taking due account of the need to identify the outcomes sought, and the best way to achieve them. But, if we are simply unable to deal with a sudden surge of emotion or a 'red-mist' that descends over our eyes, then how can we hope to instil confidence and trust in our stability and even-handedness in others? If we cannot control ourselves, why should we expect others to trust us to lead them well?

A competent leader learns to discern the strengths and weaknesses found in others. With practice and focus it is possible to recognise the triggers in everyday life that cause blinkers to drop over *our* eyes and carry us away on a surge of feelings. I clearly remember how certain managers, reporting an event and needing the legitimacy of my support, would tend to polarise their portrayal, suggesting that the situation was more 'black and white' than it really was. On the basis of their view alone it would be very easy to succumb to some sense of 'righteous indignation' or the opportunity to 'exercise my powers of judgement' summarily. But experiences learned long before holding any position of leadership served me well. As soon as anyone began to use emotive language, or I felt the picture was becoming black and white, an internal alarm invariably went off in my head, and it was as though a small voice within 'applied the brake', urging 'caution' in bright red letters!

Invariably, upon closer investigation, I found that there was at least one and sometimes many other sides to the story. Remember, the presenter of *any* such case has an agenda.

'Know thyself' is a dictum that has echoed down the ages and its relevance to all, and especially the contemporary leader, is no less now than when it was first uttered.

It is rare for the leader to find themselves 'in extremis', as did Shackleton who, with his ship crushed and sinking beneath him, ordered his men onto the ice with all they could salvage from the ship. In such situations a firm decision must be made as soon as the dangers are assessed. For most leaders, however, the pressure to make a decision or judgement is rarely as pressing as they and sometimes others with an agenda might suggest. It can be a worthwhile tactic to absorb what can be learned about the issue and then to walk away, take several deep breaths and consider the options.

If someone is pressing for or suggesting a decision be made immediately it is always worth asking yourself, at least, what the source of urgency is. Often such urgency is founded upon a desire, conscious or otherwise, to avoid the 'dilution' that time, further facts or personal reflection may well bring.

Conflict, negotiation and competition go hand in hand, and it can be useful to think of these three in terms of how they can inform each other; the questions they give rise to can be a powerful starting point in addressing conflict. If two parties are in conflict then there is invariably some disagreement in perception, definition or interpretation of a situation or issue. As a result the contrasting 'realities' require negotiation skills in seeking to reconcile differences and bring about some degree of mutuality.

Key to this process is the need to understand the benefits of a win–win outcome over one resulting in a 'winner and a loser'. The latter scenario always leaves a 'sting' of recrimination and resentment that simply sets the scene for the re-eruption of the conflict at a later date in potentially even more damaging circumstances.

Of course, not all conflicts can be resolved amicably and it would be naïve to think otherwise. Nonetheless, seeking a win–win scenario through negotiation and mutual compromise yields a more lasting settlement for all concerned.

On one occasion I was called upon to take action when an agent had been suspected of arriving at work under the influence of alcohol on several occasions. In the discussion that followed I brought some pressure to bear in exploring the reasons why this had happened, and the implications it had in the workplace of a call centre. It soon became clear that the individual had indeed been drinking heavily, and whilst the reasons given for this were in some ways understandable I found myself obliged by organisational policy to have them taken off the phones, and put on 'gardening leave', pending a doctor's report.

In this I sought to identify if the causes could be addressed and suitable treatment administered. After all, if it could be shown that the problem was a direct result of their employment it would not have sat well with any subsequent tribunal if I had not sought to identify and remedy this. Unfortunately, at this point I found myself subjected to a tirade from the individual as my being personally 'responsible' for creating hardship for their family. I was quite upset by this at the time, as on one level the threat my own action presented to his livelihood was real. On reflection, however, I realised that any guilt rightly lay with him or elsewhere. All I could do was to seek to help the person concerned reach a position where they could be reinstated.

With the application of emotional maturity, disciplinary situations can be managed and led in a way that avoids precipitate judgements and inappropriate leadership responses.

Another benefit of this 'measured approach' is that the separation of a person and their behaviour is ensured. When poor performance is conflated and confused to suggest the person is 'poor', rather than their behaviour, then their recovery or any form of 'redemption' is made un-necessarily difficult. An individual may be brought to a place where they accept their behaviour or performance was unacceptable, or below par, far more readily than they will agree to any suggestion that they themselves are in some way intrinsically 'bad' or inadequate.

Disciplinary events can actually be embraced as an opportunity to affirm and reaffirm the individual's value to the company or as a member of a team. A competent and informed leader should have little difficulty identifying positive behaviours, performance or qualities in the individual concerned and this, not the failure, should be used as a foundation for future expectation and objective-setting. An experience shared by many motorists, cyclists and skiers is one of seeing an obstacle ahead and concentrating with all their might on not hitting it. Unfortunately, the very preoccupation with the obstacle and focus upon it can lead us inexorably, it seems, to hitting it. In gymnastics it has been noted that the body tends to follow where the head points or looks; like the individual told repeatedly not to do a particular thing, it is extremely difficult to concentrate on not doing something without the very fact of our focusing upon it affecting us in some way.

The power of positivity and optimism to deal with change, conflict and failure

To the cynic, the optimist is naïve, misguided or both. Not surprisingly, though, it is the optimists in life who achieve extraordinary things. The choice is ever present in every context and situation: to see the worst or the best in people and circumstance. One is dispiriting and dis-empowering, whereas the other enervates and empowers.

How often and how easy it is to find oneself beset or undermined by negative perceptions, whether of our own construction or others. But the choice is inalienably our own. From an early age we condition ourselves to see change and circumstances as limiting, whereas in reality they invariably present new opportunities. Millions of people have found their job made redundant only to go on to greater things; others, letting themselves be governed by disappointment or a sense of failure, fail to see the freedoms and opportunities such a situation can bring.

When a change occurs that we perceive as being in some way negative or bad, it is an excellent exercise to take a moment to consider and to identify concretely the opportunities it creates.

It is this faculty that lies at the core of our ability to adapt, survive and thrive. This is worthy of long and serious consideration and reflection by all who wish to become competent leaders.

In his book *Defeat into Victory*, Field Marshall Sir William Slim's memoirs recount his time leading the British 'Burma campaign' against the Japanese during the Second World War. He found himself unexpectedly thrust into the forefront of a battle where, in the early days, he admits to committing what, on reflection, he recognises as a series of inexcusable errors. One example of these was that he 'held back' his offensive whilst striving to maximise and co-ordinate disparate forces over a large region; to 'have collected the whole strength of my corps before I attempted any counter offensive.' (p. 121).

Slim acknowledged that greater boldness in those early days would likely have saved many lives in the long run. He relates the self-doubts that assailed him in this realisation. 'Defeat is bitter. Bitter to the common soldier but trebly bitter to his general'. It must have been an agonising realisation for him to know that lives had been lost through his own failed judgement; some of the dead he undoubtedly knew personally, men who had looked to his leadership in trust, and paid for it with their lives. At this point many would balk at their apparent inability to secure the victory that Slim knew was a duty with 'no other comparable to it'.

If, at this crucial point, Slim had simply given into these misgivings and gnawing self-doubts, then the outcome of the war in Burma and Japan, and its attendant effects elsewhere, may have been very different. But taking counsel of his fears and his experience, Slim's response was anything but defeatist. His own words relating his thoughts in this dark hour can teach the contemporary leader much as they too face inevitable conflicts, adversity and personal failure:

He will see himself for what he is – a defeated General. In a dark hour he will turn in upon himself and question the very foundations of his leadership and his manhood.

And he must stop! For if he is ever to command in battle again, he must shake off these regrets, and stamp on them, as they claw at his will and his self confidence. He must beat off these attacks he delivers against himself, and cast out the doubts born of failure. Forget them, and remember only the lessons to be learnt from defeat – they are more than from victory.

Reflecting upon the vivid coverage of the gruelling challenges faced by Dame Ellen Macarthur off Antarctica, the affecting honesty of her emotions as she sought to deal with failures in her own judgement and abilities, one can find many resonances with Slim's experience. But what is transcendent is the resilience born of self-discipline each, in their own way, exemplifies, as they 'press-on' despite adversity. Field Marshall Sir William Slim went on to lead the British to a resounding victory. Reflecting the character of the man, I can also offer a personal anecdote. As a member of the Royal Signals in Burma, my father was on gatehouse duty late one night when a knock came at the small hatch which opened onto the jungle road beyond. Sliding it open my father found a diminutive Indian in a British uniform asking for the gate to be opened. From his limited viewpoint my father could only see the bright lights of a vehicle some yards away from the entrance. My father, as was his duty, requested the password and then, as the Indian soldier was unable to offer it, he refused point blank to open the gate, and closed the hatch.

In the following moments my father must have wondered whether he should call out the guard and inform the 'officer of the watch' of the nocturnal visitor. But before he could take any such action there was another and more peremptory knock on the hatch. Somewhat cautiously now, my father edged up to the hatch to avoid, as he recounted to me, any weapon that might be thrust through as he opened it, and slid the hatch to one side. Edging carefully forward he adjusted his line of sight through the hatch until he could see what lay beyond. He found himself looking not down at the diminutive Indian but rather straight at the large, broad and uniformed chest of a rather senior officer ... and more medal ribbons than he had ever seen on one uniform. At this point, the person beyond the hatch suddenly bent down and, peering at my father with what he described as 'a good humoured, mischievous expression, and a twinkle in his eye', Field Marshall Sir William Slim simply said: '*Now*, may I come in?'

For my father it was an abiding memory that he doubtless recounted to many of his comrades in arms. 'No swaggering self-importance there', he would say, 'the man knew I was doing my duty, and respected that, no matter the inconvenience to him and despite the responsibilities and cares he must have carried upon his shoulders.'

I had cause to remember this experience on many occasions, leading a busy call centre. It would be all too easy to sweep from one meeting to another with one's mind ever racing ahead over the heads of the agents on the phones I walked past, or sparing no time to acknowledge those around me. With over a thousand people working under my leadership it was vital to remember that eye contact or a passing word of encouragement would provide a subject for often greater reflection on their part than one might think it merited. But that is the way of it. It does matter. As with other areas of leadership such as communication it is not only the merits of doing something that should be taken into account but also the penalties for not doing so. As described earlier, the effect of the new Operation Manager filled with self-importance striding across the office without a glance to left or right left behind him a wake of discouragement and antipathy.

In conclusion, conflict and adversity are not something the competent leader shies away from. Given that the leader's role is one of driving change and of ever questioning the value and effectiveness of the status quo, it is a contradiction in terms to think they might simply be avoided, or they are somehow a deviation from the norm in the leader's life. It is for this reason that I have emphasised the need for any aspiring leader to prepare for these challenges. It begins with learning to 'lead yourself', and this requires the development of self-discipline as a core competence of every leader as an individual.

Self-discipline is the mortar holding together the leader's sense of self and purpose when conflict and adversity arise. It is not a characteristic that develops of its own accord. It must be nurtured and encouraged. With practice one learns to identify the onset of those moments when desire to reach an objective begins to falter; when the inner voices urging rest or querying our ability rise from the shadows, and doubts crowd in. It is precisely at these moments that our ability to make a conscious decision 'despite' how we may feel makes the difference. Like any muscle or a habit, self-discipline grows stronger through exercise, and weaker through indolence and apathy.

Finally, the great leaders are those who, in the face of apparently overwhelming odds, choose to go on, despite there being no apparent hope of success or even survival. When the chips are down, as they were so clearly for Field Marshall Sir William Slim, Sir Ernest Shackleton or Dame Ellen Macarthur, *that* is where the self-discipline of true leadership really shows its mettle.

10

Landfall and reflections in still waters

With good fortune and good leadership practice, a moment finally arrives when it becomes apparent that ends sought will indeed be achieved. I distinctly remember a moment in the course of those 7 weeks I had to set up a call centre when, for no apparent reason, I became aware that even if I vanished from the process, and all things being equal, the call centre would open on time. It was a pivotal point for me, as I realised that I had successfully communicated my vision and how it might be realised to every member of the team. Not only that, but I had also been able to communicate sufficient understanding that everyone involved could now make decisions without, in the most part, recourse to me. The 'exceptions', I knew, would only arise if something unforeseeable arose, as I had discussed foreseeable 'contingencies' and planned for them.

It is a good position to achieve, being on top of the curve, because it affords an opportunity to look ahead and anticipate what does or may lie ahead. I have already discussed the organisation benefits of making oneself redundant and succession management but there is, too, a danger inherent in this approach that the leader does well to take account of.

At this point one may likely feel inclined to 'sit back and coast', take time out to relax and slowly thereby become complacent, such that one fails to notice small signals forewarning difficulties ahead.

By now we should recognise that although things may be going according to plan, and the organisational momentum towards our desired objectives, however measured, is such that it requires little direct intervention on our part, other forces are invariably at work. The environment in which we operate is constantly changing, and the competent leader will invariably take this time to consider if targets, the means to their objective and the ability of the organisation to meet them remain relevant and appropriate. Furthermore, this is the time when ever greater efforts should be directed to identifying ways by which the organisational structures and processes can be improved, both in their own right and also to anticipate identified or possible changes, whether they are internal or external.

The competent leader is never complacent; their eye must ever be switching between the horizon and what is before them, ever attuned to 'changes in the wind, weather, clouds and waves, as well as the expressions and demeanour of their crew, the seaworthiness of their vessel and the quality and quantity of their provisions'.

Beyond loneliness

When Tony Blair took over as Prime Minister he found a message waiting for him on a table in 10 Downing Street when he entered for the first time. It was from John Major, the outgoing PM. It simply said: 'It's a lonely job'.

Owning two Siberian huskies, I was fairly horrified to learn how Shackleton's sled dog handlers had to endure the ordeal of seeing their canine companions 'put-down' and cooked for food. That it was necessary to carry out the task

I cannot know at such a remove from their dire predicament, but it seems likely. Had Shackleton been a dog-lover, or formed a close bond with them, his ability to make an objective decision bearing upon the welfare of the entire crew would have been so much the harder.

As a leader I was keenly aware that wider organisational demands in its competitive and 'political' environment might at any time require me to 'lose' some members of staff, or even to close down the entire centre and make everyone redundant. In 'everyone', I include, of course, those who worked closest to me, and in whom I might confide more than most.

This knowledge alone was sufficient for me to recognise the need to maintain some distance between me and those I led. Apart from any other consideration, my allowing them to get 'too close' would further emphasise any sense of betrayal and guilt that 'letting them go' would likely entail. It was not a comfortable knowledge, but was nevertheless a necessary consideration in a commercial environment. I also knew that I personally was not exempt from the vagaries of organisational life. Ultimately, as I would soon discover, my role could be deemed expendable, and, perhaps ironically, my own departure might well be deemed beneficial.

Two specific experiences brought home the distance necessary between the leader and those they lead in my direct experience as call-centre manager. One arose when one of my operation managers was accused of 'minor sexual harassment' – this, as it turned out, was largely a matter of perception and interpretation on the part of the accusers rather than anything 'physical'. Of course, had I been 'too close' to the manager concerned, I would have found my ability to act as an objective and fair arbiter in the matter so much more difficult.

In another example, my role obliged me to carry out regular performance reviews with my immediate managers. Again, had I been overly 'familiar' with them, then this too might have presented real problems had they been poor performers but a 'good friend'.

Ultimately, there is no way around it. For the aspiring competent leader, there must be a genuine acceptance of the isolation and burden of loneliness that comes with the mantle of leadership.

At the same time, however, the result of this self-imposed 'separation' can often result in the very human need to find a way or person with whom we feel able to unburden ourselves. This often takes place through a caring partner, workplace mentor, external activity, group or even religion, where frustrations and tensions can be vented harmlessly. In any case, it is as well to be aware that the inevitable frustrations and pressures of leadership need to be monitored in their cumulative ability to affect our own judgement, patience and performance.

Like 'hypothermia – where exposure to prolonged cold can cause a drift into sleep from which there is no awakening – so too the stress of command can develop insidiously, just below the threshold of conscious awareness, and the more we focus on the job at hand, the easier it becomes to take less and less account of our own internal state and 'objectivity'.

As a competent leader we must nevertheless take time out to monitor the degree of stress we are under, and to note, through reflexivity, if we begin to act or think in ways we know indicate a deviation from the norm for us. Even if there is no immediate confidante for us to turn to, some awareness of being on edge can at least help us guard against impulsive stress-driven reactions. I learned to make a point of 'making space' for myself by literally taking a short walk from time to time. I also learned to monitor my breathing – a few long slow deep breaths in the fresh air can have a startling impact on our mood and perceptions.

Much of our consideration of practical leadership focuses on the aspiring competent leader's personal willingness to embrace and develop key qualities of self-discipline, reflexivity and objectivity. But the bald exhortation that one should simply 'be' a certain way may often leave one with an abyss to cross, but no apparent wherewithal to do so.

I found drawing upon the example of great leaders to be tremendously helpful – not least because this provided a real counter to any sense of loneliness: the paths I trod, no matter how difficult, were well trodden by countless others before me. Another great source of comfort and inspiration was of course my unwitting mentor, Kate.

It was quite by accident that I stumbled upon the relevance of Joseph Campbell's insights into ancient world mythology for practical leadership. Through his work I came to appreciate that what takes place between characters in the mythical world often mirrors those occurring in one's inner landscape. The archetypal roles of King, Warrior, Jester and Wise Man: all inhabit each individual as aspects of their character. I found value in this insight as a leader for I realised I have need of each of these characteristics from time to time. When in doubt and uncertainty, it may be to the inner voice of any of these aspects of our nature that we may profitably turn to for counsel (Wise Man), integrity (King or Queen), strength (Warrior) or perspective (Jester), etc.

Some may shy away from or resist such a focus on the internal life of the leader. Yet if it is true that competent leadership is nurtured and sustained by self-discipline and reflexivity in particular then anything that may cast light on our inner world and encourages or inspires us is to be valued. It is, after all, precisely this inner world from which the leader's motivation to lead, to be inspired and inspire others through vision and encouragement arises.

For that abyss between what we are and what we aspire to to be bridged, a useful starting point can be to recognise, in our own personal experience, moments when our inner King/Queen, Jester or Warrior has arisen unbidden within us. It may have been when we went against some tide of opinion, when we discovered and tapped into a strength we were unaware we possessed, or, in the case of the Jester, the moment when all seemed to be at its most grim yet we found the strength to laugh out loud, and by doing so inadvertently gained a fresh, broader perspective on things, as well as feeling all the better for it.

In the development of inner strength, these voices of 'ancient experience' can be tremendously empowering. Just being able to remember to recall, especially when we feel weak and unworthy, what we felt in success – albeit momentarily to re-immerse ourselves in that remembrance – can in itself be enough to shake the fetters that limit our perspective, hiding our view of 'the wood' and its end, by limiting our perception to individual trees.

I was fortunate to remain in contact with quite a few colleagues from my early days as leader and eventually, with some trepidation, I sought their assessment of my leadership based on the benefit that time and their subsequent experience offered.

I was reassured by the positive feedback I received from people no longer influenced, to some greater or lesser degree, by their 'working for me'. Nevertheless, there were some surprises: aspects of my performance and ability I was aware of but believed others had no cause or reason to notice or be aware of.

Principal among these was a tendency to exhibit a degree of 'tunnel vision' when the pressure was on that took the form of my becoming more single minded and less open to debate. Single-mindedness is understandable, but recognise too that this, in some ways positive characteristic, carries the inherent danger of not listening to others enough.

I also realised through this frank exchange that however well one performs in their role, and however highly they may be regarded, every weakness is noted. But it was also heartening to realise that good staff will put up with such foibles if they are confident, despite them, that you hold their interests dear and your overall credibility remains sound.

No matter how much respect one is afforded or how much support is received, leadership remains a fundamentally lonely road. Many a 'spin' can be put on the most innocuous of actions or comments on your part. You are in the 'public eye' in the eyes of your team as much as any celebrity pursued by the paparazzi. Whether you are a man or woman, your every gaze and comment will be open to all manner of speculation as to possible interpretation or implication. The pursuit for knowledge of the person behind the title is relentless. Every aspiring leader should be prepared for this. Knowledge is certainly power; you may be certain that disclosures about your personal life are likely to become common knowledge sooner or later and may subsequently be used against you when the clouds lower, the storm rises and your credibility or motives are questioned.

11

Epilogue

In all that has been discussed about leadership much has been offered to expose as an illusion the notion that leadership is glamorous, or a clear-cut matter of following formulae offered by textbooks or case studies. The closest I have been able to come to developing a successful model for dealing with the complexities of leadership is reflected in my 'four questions'. They have unerringly guided and informed me whenever I have faced uncertainty. In the end, leading others through uncertainty, especially that thrown up by change, as is the focus of most leadership activity, is what practical leadership is all about. If we cannot frame questions to challenge the organisational inertia or momentum in which we work, then we cannot change anything.

Nevertheless, the fortunes of the leader on their never-ending journey to competence may rise and fall regardless of performance or expectation.

A few months after taking over and 'turning around' a call centre that was staggering under the client's accusation of a 'breach of contract' on grounds of poor quality, my role was made redundant.

Despite having succeeded in leadership in terms of performance, from the point of view of both client and employer, I found myself walking out of the call centre for the last time, without a job, and all that meant for me personally. The reason for this unexpected and most unwelcome turn of events was that the client was instructed by their overseas owner to re-in-source all their call centres. Simultaneously, my own employer was approached by another larger client and told their provision of my call centre constituted a 'conflict of interest' for them: lose my client, or lose their more lucrative business.

Ultimately the competent leader learns to treat such vagaries of fortune with equanimity. In doing so, one moves forward enriched and stronger for the experience. Little in life or leadership is certain, but those who learn from experience rather than being embittered by it, or avoiding its challenges, fare far better. The abiding stories of their lives, their leadership and all who follow in their footsteps are so much the richer and better for it.

Index

Printed in the United Kingdom
by Lightning Source UK Ltd.
109995UKS00001B/41